Life Lessons
for My Black Girls

Life Lessons
for My Black Girls

*How to Make Wise Choices
and Live a Life You Love!*

by

Natasha Munson

toExcel

San Jose   New York   Lincoln   Shanghai

Life Lessons for My Black Girls
How to Make Wise Choices and Live a Life You Love!

Published by toExcel, an imprint of iUniverse.com, Inc.

For information, please contact:
iUniverse.com, Inc.
620 North 48th St., Suite 201
Lincoln, NE 68504
www.iuniverse.com

ISBN: 1-58348-521-X

Printed in the United States of America

Dedication

This is for you my precious black girls, especially my beautiful daughters Mecca and Kenya, and my "little" cousins Tiffany and Monique.

Here is what I wish
that you hold true to yourself
it is not selfish to love yourself
more than any other
it is the pillar of self-esteem
focus on your goals and ambitions
understand though that destiny
must be confronted
when you feel you have strayed from the path
know that at this time you are gaining strength
often referred to as experience
accept it and your goals will stay sharp
demand respect or it will not be given
uphold your honest mind
letting only the truth be your guide
then you will never have to watch your back
or remember what you said
hate no one due to color
always judge by states of mind
color is just like looks
it can be deceiving

always question your surroundings
answer your whys
acceptance too soon can enslave your mind
understand that spirituality is the glue
that holds you together
belief in God can get you through a lot
that is where your faith should lie
trust no one more than yourself
depend on yourself first
love yourself first
respect yourself
encourage yourself
be happy with yourself
then share that love

Preface

I don't know the father of my children. I mean, I don't know who he is anymore. When we met I thought he was wonderful. You could feel the energy of love in the air. I thanked God for bringing him into my life. I later found out that he thanked God that night too.

We talked so much, every night, since the first date. We talked for hours! We were so in sync, so right for one another. We became a couple. He was loving and sweet and considerate. He would call just to say, "Did I tell you I loved you today?" I remember how special that made me feel, because I felt I had found someone special. I knew his goals, dreams, fears, nightmares. I knew what type of father he would be. I knew the man he would become and the type of husband he would be.

Then, within a year and a half, our relationship began to fade away. I saw that he wasn't the man I wanted. He wasn't the man I could love forever. There was something tearing him away from me.

I cried many nights when I realized he didn't love himself as much as I loved him. My heart felt like it would break when I waited in the window wondering where he was. It hurt my heart when I found out that this guy I thanked God for had lost his soul and desire to crack. There was nothing I could do to bring him back. Not crying, loving, screaming or fighting. Nothing.

My being pregnant just sent him further away and sent me within myself, wondering where I had gone wrong. He began to look like a person without a soul. His eyes looked like glass. I couldn't see the love in them anymore. The person I loved was no longer in that body. The windows of his soul had closed and kicked me out.

Now, though I see him when the kids go to their grandparents, I don't know him. I don't know who he is or what he stands for. All I see is a shell of a guy I thought had so much potential to be a great man.

My love blinded me, but my spirit saved me. My spirit pulled me through that torment so I could regain my life and stop trying to save him.

The greatest lessons I've learned from him is that love is beautiful, but you must know if that love is genuine. You have to know if he truly loves you or just truly needs to be loved. I also learned that actions are so much stronger than words. We have to do what we say we are going to do. Our intentions are nothing if we don't follow up with action.

Getting through this relationship involved a lot of introspection. I looked at myself a lot. I wondered how I got myself into this situation and how I was going to get out of it. I went through the gamut of emotions. I blamed myself for not seeing him for what he really was. I thought I was stupid. I thought I would never love anyone again because I just didn't know how to choose men and now I was a single parent.

Then at some point I remembered what my friend Kevin had said to me once. He said, "Tasha, don't ever let anyone kill your spirit. That's the most beautiful thing about you." I thought of him being open enough to tell me that and I cried. I cried because I had let my life become a rut. I allowed myself to focus on this dead end relationship. I was killing myself. I knew I wasn't being Tasha anymore, I was being pitiful, so I changed.

I knew I could rely on myself to get out of the rut. I knew my spirit was too strong and that there was much more I could accomplish in life. So I began slowly to live my life. But it was that relationship that changed me into the spiritual person I am now. It allowed me to feel appreciation and love for those that were caring and loving towards me. It gave me humility and showed me my strength. That relationship, though painful, changed my life.

Now I know we can't all just change. I do know that prior to this relationship I had very high self-esteem and regard for myself. I loved myself more than anyone in this world and knew without a doubt that no one was better than me. So I simply had to remember what I knew.

That foundation I had was given to me by God. But everyday I see women hurting and dealing with relationships that are killing their spirit and I wish I could say something. I wish I could tell each and every one of them to stop and live for themselves. Everyone should know that they are the best in this world, they are a gift from God.

We should all know that we are going to make mistakes. But that does not make us stupid, that makes us human. We are all going to face obstacles and challenges, we just need to know how to deal with them. We all need to know how to tap into life and live it to its fullest. We need to know that God is within us.

When I was coming back to my senses I decided to share my experiences. I wanted to alleviate some of the pain others were going through and share my knowledge. I wanted to help others love themselves. I decided to write something for my daughters: a little manual of things I think they should know, a guide that would tell them what I had gone through and what others have gone through so they could learn some lessons. I also wanted a way of telling them things that aren't so easy to say face to face.

So many of our young girls are misguided and uninformed, especially about sex and relationships. We have to speak to them. We have to prepare them. We cannot pretend forever that they are cute little girls. They will be women soon enough and the more preparation we give them, the more they will know. An informed woman is powerful. So my goal is to tell them the truth about life, the lessons I have learned, and the universal lessons black women have learned.

Contents

"Love Yourself"

"Live in Love"

"Shape your life"

"Use your resources"

"Keep your freedom"

Introduction

Life Lessons for My Black Girls

How to Make Wise Choices and Live a Life You Love!

This book is meant to be a resource—your personal guide through life. I want to tell you what I know, honestly and openly, so that you can experience a more fulfilling life. I know that everyone in the world has an opinion for you. They tell you who you are and who you should be. I want to break it down and let you design your life, for yourself, and your own personal happiness.

This is definitely not the be all and end all. You are not going to receive everything you need to know about life in this handy dandy book. But you will be equipped with the knowledge you need to make wise decisions and live life to the fullest.

I am going to deal with many topics. I'm still relatively young myself, so I haven't been through everything. But a lot of stuff does happen in your twenties, let me tell you! So, I made sure this book contains some advice, quotes and poems that will inspire you, motivate you and get you out there living life. Did I mention it will also help you make wise decisions?

God knows life should come with a study guide. Now here's yours, from me with love, and the hope that it creates a life more wonderful and fulfilling than you could ever have imagined.

"Create Your Life"

"This is your life and you determine the outcome."

*Time is of the essence
when you're reaching for that dream
every decision matters
like signs in the road
guiding you
on your journey
think clearly
notice every subtle clue
let your spirit be your guide
to a life filled with love
find what you love to do
and do it well*

All your life you have been something, someone's child, someone's granddaughter, someone's friend. But now it is time to separate yourself and find out who you are. All teenagers go through a period of getting to know themselves. Some twenty-year olds are still doing it. And older! But this time really is meant for you to stretch your spirit and learn about your purpose in life.

Right now you are very good at comparing. You know you're nothing like so-and-so, or you would never do this or that. These are the things I want you to tap into. Who are you? Think about some of the situations your friends or your family are in. Would you deal with the same situation? Why not? What about you makes you different? Would you stay with a guy who cheated on you? A guy who called you names? Would you stay with a guy who had no money? Why?

Make a list right now of the things you simply would not tolerate. This list describes your character. This is who you are and what you represent. You want this list to be truly reflective of you, so think of every possible situation you can. Think of the things you don't want to happen in your life. If you know you don't want to be a single parent, write that down. Write down the reason why not.

Then write a realistic dream wish list. A realistic dream wish list contains things you definitely want to happen in your life. So begin with your dreams. What is your biggest wish? What is your dream? Describe your dream life. Then, add the "realistic" side, the things you will have to do to make those dreams a reality.

Now look at your two lists. What you have done is describe the person you are and the person you will become. Nothing on the lists are impossible. You can make everything happen that you want to, and you will. All you have to do is turn each dream into realistic steps.

Every dream you have is a whisper from God. It's your destiny. All you have to do is begin the journey. All you have to do to achieve what you want in life is know that God believes in you. God gave you the dream. All you have to do is make it become reality.

Now you may say well, that's a big dream. Please! God created the universe. Your dream to become the next astronaut is not impossible. Don't think you are limited. Use your mind to your advantage and don't let anyone discourage you. No matter what happens in your life, keep your realistic dream wish list and work on it. You owe it to yourself to find inner happiness.

Lesson: This is your life and you determine the outcome. No one can live your life for you. The best thing you can do for yourself and for others is to live your life. When you are happy with your life and your life choices you pass that happiness on just by being yourself. So each day remember you are special. Each day be true to yourself. And most importantly, each day work towards making your realistic dream wish list a reality.

Listening to the opinion of others

On the 21st is when
a man becomes a man
and a woman becomes a woman
but time will tell
that the mind is not always even
with the physical
so how do things lie
when age is no longer equated
with wisdom

Opinions, opinions, opinions. Everyone has one. Everyone thinks he or she knows exactly what you should do with your life. In their defense, they can see your life more objectively than you can. They can see what mistakes you've made and can possibly perceive of mistakes you are about to make. But opinions are not dependable. You know why; because everyone has one. So everyone you listen to can give you a different perspective of your life. They say, well, if I were you I would do this.

If you want even a shred of happiness in this life, remember what they're saying and look at the underlying message: they are not you. That's why this is *your* life. So the decision you have to make is going to have to come from you. You know what's best for you. You just have to know that the advice you give yourself is the only advice you need.

I firmly believe that God talks to us through our intuition. You know that little voice that tells you what is right or wrong, whether you should do something or not. That is God, utilizing your unconscious to guide you in your life. And, all you have to do is listen.

It is essential to your life that you listen to that little voice and know when to tune out the opinions of others.

Lesson: The best opinion is your opinion. Do not be afraid to make decisions for yourself.

"Education Unlocks Your Destiny."

*The difference
between the height
of achievement
and the level
of mediocrity
is entirely
one of decision*

I know when you hear this you tend to tune out. You think, yeah, education is everything and a mind is a terrible thing to waste. I have no intention of wasting my mind so I guess I'm a step ahead and yadda yadda yadda. But let me tell you, education is much more important than you can ever imagine. Education unlocks your destiny. That means what you put into your education is what you will get out of life.

In determining your educational pattern (college, trade school, or business venture), you have to decide first where you want to be in life. You have to realistically think about what you want to do. What will your impact be in this life? You cannot live life through others or for others. So the best decision you can make is to take your education seriously. Study as if your life depended on it. As much interest as you take in your looks and your clothes, make sure you are doubly interested in your education.

What is education? Education is a learning experience that changes your outlook or thinking pattern. Education can make a fundamental difference in your life.

To make the best educational choice after high school ask some friends and family members what they think your strengths and weaknesses are. You will be amazed at how well some people can define you and pinpoint things in yourself that you hadn't noticed. Once you hear what they believe your strengths are, think about their opinion. What do the strengths say about your character? What type of career can you see yourself in with these types of strengths? Remember not to limit yourself. There are more opportunities then being a nurse or a lawyer. Open your mind to the many career possibilities. The goal is to find something you love to do, not something you have to do.

If you could be anything, what would you be? No, not rich! What would you be doing? Great, that's your goal, that's your dream. Now you have to make that a reality. It is your responsibility, not your mom's, not your pop's, to find out how to make your dream come true. So write down what your dream job would be. Then think of ways that dream could become a reality. Do you need to attend college? Do you need money to start? What do you realistically need? Do you need a mentor, someone who has been there, done that? Think of every possible way to make your dreams happen. Even if they feel unrealistic and farfetched now, write them down. You are on your way to happiness.

Once you have a list of what you can do to make your dream become reality, the next step is something many people never do. You have to start. You have to pick something on that list and make it become reality. Whether it's approaching a businesswoman and asking if she can mentor you or whether it's attending a workshop—make it happen!

Lesson: Take education seriously and fulfill it. It is the catalyst to changing your life and making your dreams reality. If you want a better life, you have to study and work toward it.

"Be the Chooser, Not the Chosen."

I say this is my life
and you stop telling me what to do
I say this is my life
and you stop telling me what to do
I say this is MY life
and you stop telling me what to do
No I'm not whining
I'm trying to get through
this is my life
and I run this show
this is my life
and I know
what I want
I don't need you to tell me
I feel it in my heart
I'm on a mission
please don't stand in my way
this is my life
and I must run it
so that I may love it

If you let it happen, life will take control of you. Things will happen in your life and you will have no control. You will simply go from job to job, man to man, situation to situation, because you are allowing others to dictate your life. All your life people have been telling you what to do. Your parents, your grandparents, your friends—they have all given you advice on what to do with your life. And you have listened because you know they meant well. But what you are going to have to do now, is listen to yourself.

I know that every person was put here to fulfill a spiritual purpose. We all have something to contribute to this life. What you have to do is listen to your inner voice. You know that voice that tells you what's right and wrong for you. Listen. Please listen.

That little voice is the best gift you have. That little voice is your intuition. Intuition is God. This is how he talks to you. You have a direct connection with the most powerful force in the universe. You can tap into that power at any time, with any question, and you will be guided to the right answer for you. There is nothing outside of yourself, not friends or family that can answer better than that little voice.

Your little voice is your spiritual guide. It will help you to make decisions and live life to the fullest. This is what you want. You want to live life to the fullest. The last thing you want to do is be unhappy, right? So let me tell you again, LISTEN.

Listening to your inner voice, your intuition, gives you the power of God. In essence you have the power to create your life. Remember what I said, *you have the power to create your life.* Every decision you make determines your future. From picking the right boyfriend to the best school, each decision is a turning point in your life.

Think of your decisions as signs along the road. Your destination is happiness and success. So your decision-making is extremely important. Number one: you have to know where you're going. Where do you want to be? Number two: you have to think of the best route. Number three: when there's an obstacle, and there will be obstacles, you have to think of another way to get there.

Understand that life isn't meant to be difficult; it's meant to be a learning experience. The decisions and choices you make determine what you will learn. Your response to the obstacles you are confronted with will determine whether you settle and become complacent or whether you keep going.

Lesson: Make every decision as if your life depended on it. One day you will see, your life, your happiness, your success, depends on the decisions and choices you make.

Getting caught up in day-to-day life

What ever happened to that dream
that was deferred
was it bought off
like the people in this land
or did it sit and become glop
to be eaten by the neverminds
and won;t works
was that dream ever real
or in fact a true case
of figment of the imagination

Once you get out of the house and are on your own, it is very easy to get caught up in life. You get accustomed to paying the bills, maybe seeing a movie, hanging out with the girls, spending time with your man, and this cycle of redundancy will continue for as long as you let it. Let me just tell you, it is easy to become stagnant.

You can have hopes, dreams and goals but if you allow yourself to get caught up in day-to-day drama, all your ambitions will seem less attainable. You have to give yourself and the pursuit of your dreams top priority. This is not to say that your loved ones aren't important. This is just to state that, in your life, you are your top priority. And, believe me, there is nothing wrong with putting yourself first.

I'm not saying be selfish and be all about me, me, me. But definitely give yourself time to live. Realistically, you only get one shot at this life. The decisions you make each and every day will determine the outcome of your life. Do you really want your day-to-day struggle to be the pinnacle of your life? Believe me, no one ever said, damn, that girl ain't never do nothing with her life but she sure could pay some bills! The only person focusing on your bills is you and you're going to have to shift that focus to getting out of the rut, living life, and making your dreams happen.

Remember, the only things that stay constant are the things that you allow to remain constant. Give yourself a break, all right. Live life.

Lesson: Whatever you focus on is what you will have and what you will get. If you want more out of life, focus your energy and time to achieving that. Visualize the life you want and make it happen. Let someone else focus on the day-to-day drama.

"Know Yourself"

The Ideal Man

His spirit is so strong
yet gentle enough
to share
to laugh
to hold
to be with

he is sweet
and considerate
in a way that is so loving
and so supportive
you feel like you've know him
all your life

he is reliable

finally someone
who meets the definition of man
he's the one women dream about
and here he is
with a smile
that makes your heart melt

eyes of wonder

and sensuality

and an embrace

that makes you feel like gold

but really

he's the gem

If you look at books and television, women everywhere are looking for Mr. Right. They're fighting over him, sharing him, stealing him, doing everything they can to get him. And who is he? Who is Mr. Right? Well, if he's your Mr. Right you won't have to fight, lie, steal, or cheat to get him. He will be right there in your life at the right time. When or if he will enter your life is totally on you.

Before you go on your search for Mr. Right, you better make sure you're Ms. Right. Sometimes we hold ourselves up to very high ideals. We envision ourselves in a way that is not totally accurate. If you don't have your stuff together, the only person that will not know is you. Everyone else knows fully that you have some issues.

The best thing you can do in this life is take some time for you. That does not mean five minutes in the bathroom. I mean take some time. Chill. Get to know yourself. See what type of person you are without a man. You never, ever, want to be in a position where you need a man. No man in this world can complete you or make your life better. Looking for a Mr. Right with money might make your financial picture better, but it's not going to change whatever issues you were dealing with before you met him. Keep it real with yourself and don't expect anyone but you to fulfill your life.

When you take time for yourself and get to know you, you bring your best self into a relationship. Because then you know you can rely on yourself, you love yourself, and you are happy with yourself. Until you can do these three things, you ain't doing nothing but wasting your time trying to find Mr. Right because you're not Ms. Right yet.

Becoming Ms. Right definitely does not mean reaching a state of perfection. No one is perfect. What it does mean though, is that you love yourself, you are not holding on to any ill feelings, you don't hate anyone, you are simply going for the best in life and willing to open yourself to loving. The ideal woman is one who realizes that this world was created for her. God gave you the world as a gift and you are a gift to this world. The ideal woman wants to make her life one of definition, where her spiritual purpose is fulfilled. She is always willing to learn and to teach. She gives of herself lovingly, but sparingly. She knows that no one in this world can fulfill her. No one can provide for her. She is here to be a partner not a dependent.

The ideal man will love you for who you are now. He will not find fault in you. He will not try to bring you down. He will be your friend, your lover, your partner.

Lesson: The ideal man is someone that complements your life and seeks to make you a better person. He is one you can love, learn, laugh, play and grow with. He is a man that will stimulate you to reach your highest goals.

"Know what you stand for."

When I keep silent
am I helping you
or hurting myself

My God knows
I am killing myself
when I don't tell you
exactly where what
when and why

I'm limiting my mind
and allowing you
to define me
when I know what I believe

holding in my words
is like holding in my breath
I will suffocate my spirit
if I don't tell you my truth

my truth is me
I am my truth
they cannot be separated
so I will speak

The quote "If you don't know what you stand for, you will fall for anything" is pure truth. In this life, you have to know what you want. You have to be able to look at yourself realistically. And, most importantly, you have to be able to look at others realistically. You have to understand the motivations and desires behind people's actions.

Many people go through life systematically. They have no desire to go beyond a specific position in life. They are comfortable. Therefore the entirety of their life is focused on the day to day issues. The focal point of their conversation is themselves or their relationships. Life beyond that does not exist or simply is not important to them. You have to realize the magnitude of that.

Thinking only of yourself and the relationship you're in limits your spirit, your growth and your life. This is your life. You have to know what you will and will not stand for. You have to want more than any other person you know. You have to want the best. Work for the best. Achieve the best. It is so important that the sooner you know what you want out of life that you immediately begin working towards it. Never forget, it's a blessing to even know what you want out of this life. It's a reward to achieve it.

Lesson: In order to have a fulfilling life and make confident, wise choices you have to know what you will and will not stand for in life. You have to be unwavering in your decision to be yourself and stand up for your truth. If you don't totally agree, you don't agree. Don't mislead or compromise yourself so that others may feel comfortable. Speak your truth, live your truth.

Overcoming Obstacles

The challenges of life are ever-changing.
When confronted with an obstacle
speak, yell, shout, push, pull, kick, hit
move the obstacle.
To do nothing
leaves you unchallenged
limited
and a fool.

Anything you allow to block your path towards greatness is an obstacle. Any person or situation that gets in your way must be removed. This does not mean you use greed or malicious means to get what you want. Rather you take the desire of a better life that exists within you and you make your dreams happen.

We are all always learning and always striving for more. You are simply just beginning. When people come to you with negative energy and negative thoughts, shake it off. Literally take a deep breath and blow it out. It's not worth it. The more you allow the opinions and thoughts of others to effect you, the longer it will take for you to achieve your dream.

Look at the motivations of others. See if they are with you or not, then make the proper decision. It is essential to know when to let people out of your life. Some people are not willing to work as hard for their goal. You have to wish them well and send them on their way. Never let anyone get between you and your dream.

There's nothing in this world more important than your happiness. Because once you've achieved a dream you will be a happier person and will be able to spread that to others. No matter what happens in life, do not let anyone deter you from achieving your dream. Your dream is your purpose in life. You have to fulfill it.

Lesson: There will be situations that seem insurmountable. There will be obstacles that you will feel are too difficult to get by. Everything you believe is true. If you believe an obstacle will remain an obstacle, it will. If you believe there is a way to get past an obstacle, you will find the way.

"Know your definition of happiness."

Even with everything
something can be missing

Your heart may long for
fulfillment

Your soul may want
to love

Your breath may need
to coincide with a loved one

The deepest moment
that which fulfills
bringing the happiness of heaven
is the love of
your soulmate

We always hear, but don't realize the magnitude, that happiness is within. I want you to listen to yourself say, happiness is within me, happiness is within me, happiness is within me. Where's happiness? Exactly, it's within you. That means that in order to be happy and fulfilled you have to fill your needs. You have to follow your heart, pursue your dreams and you have to listen to yourself. We can make some of our most foolish mistakes based on the advice of others. You have to do what feels right for you. Don't let anyone mislead you or talk you out of your dreams. Happiness is your choice. Your decisions, your choice in friends, everything will decide your happiness.

Someone once told me, misery loves company. I was like, whatever. I knew he had good intentions by trying to give me advice. But I had no idea of what he was really saying until I was out of the situation and could look back on it.

I realize now that not everyone in this world wants to be happy. That's right. People will keep themselves in the same situations and keep making the same foolish choices. Your life can go around in circles or it can keep going forward and getting better. It's all on you. This is your life.

So for your happiness, decide who you will and will not be around. Don't waste your time thinking you can change anyone in your life, especially a man. Don't love a man for his potential, love him for who he is. You will get your heart broken and maybe your wallet busted if you love a man for what he will one day become. There are some exceptions out there, I guess, but don't rely on it. Love the man for who he is now. If you can do that then you are in love. If you cannot because you're saying well, things would be better if he was just this or that—*unh unh*, get out of that situation, asap.

The way you spend your time and the people you spend that time with can directly affect your happiness. There are people who bring nothing but negative energy. We can't do this and we can't do that. You need to drop them quickfast. Then there are those sista friends that you love but, you're loving them for their potential too. Unlike our men, we give our friends more benefit of the doubt. We think they're definitely going to make it. All I can say is, don't get drawn in. Don't get caught up in the whims of others. Don't get focused on other people's problems. It's not a matter of not caring. It's a matter of self-preservation. You will lose your mind trying to figure out what some people are thinking. Girl, let the drama go. Don't let anyone add to your stress level. Anyone stressing you or constantly making you unhappy has got to go!

The reason I say most people don't want their own happiness is because at any moment everyone has the power to change their lives. It's not about actions at that point. It's about your belief system. The catalyst to changing your life lies in your attitude. Whatever you believe will be your reality. You are empowered each and every day to make this a life you will enjoy. You don't have to be miserable. You don't have to get caught up in day-to-day drama. You don't have to live paycheck to paycheck. Don't settle. Don't think you can't go any higher. You can have whatever you want in this life. You just have to believe and then place that belief system in action.

Lesson: Happiness is your choice. If you want it badly enough, you will find ways to achieve it.

"Know who you are."

Decide who you are
who you want to be
and then
do everything
in your power
to be that

Our situations and experiences define who we are. They define the way we feel, the way we react, what we want and how we live.

Experiences and our reactions to them directly define our belief system. Everything you've gone through has shaped your personality. You may have picked up some character traits from family, but you are unique. What you believe, what you want, what you will and will not expect are directly linked to what you have experienced. This is your foundation of life. This outlook will make or break you. It can leave you bitter or have you wanting to find happiness.

Life is all about what you want from it. In each and every moment you have the power to shape what you will experience. Experiences happen, but it is what we do with that experience that shapes our character. You have the power to shape your reactions. You have the power to change your belief system. It's all about your level of thinking and whether you will let yourself have control of your life or whether you will let life control you. Know who you are and realize that at all times your destiny is in your control.

Lesson: It is important to know who you are. This is your foundation of beliefs, values, and culmination of experiences that will guide you in life. If your foundation is strong, you will make wise decisions in your life. Once you are comfortable with who you are, no one can define or tell you what to do with your life. You will realize that knowing who you are and loving yourself are the keys to controlling the happiness of your life.

"Love Yourself"

A True Friend

In a world of mixture
I never know how my life will turn
what is true one minute
can soon become part of
a web of chaotic lies
the pure
polluted
the divine
questionable
or is it that life is scary
like a goldfish in the ocean
I swim constantly
sometimes upstream
sometimes in water as peaceful
as the Nile
I never know physically
where I will end up
but spiritually I've been
in heaven for many years
as my life goes on now
I hope out of all
in this world
at least one
true person
will remain in my life
I surely will smile

when someone can look me in the eye
and say I know you
and finally, I can believe them

Friendship can be a difficult thing. You think because you've known some-one for so long, that they always have your best interests at hand. Sometimes, though, they only have their interests at hand. Your personal responsibility is to make sure that the friends you have in your life are really your friends. Would this person be there for you through every up and down? Do they have your back? If you really needed the help, would she be there?

It's very easy for us to hang out and party with one another. But when the chips are down, and stuff is rough, there's only a few that will be there with you. I remember when my father told me, "You have to be careful with those you consider friends", I thought he was crazy. Now I know that friends are extensions of you. They are your family. They are supportive. They love you no matter what. They will be there for you to tell you when you're doing good and when you're doing bad. Your true friend will keep it real with you. He or she will not want anything from you, but your time. They will not steal your energy or be demanding, but will be reliable.

Hanging out with your girls is cool, but there will come a time when you're going to need a support system. The best thing you can do for yourself now is know who you can depend on and who you cannot. Once you know it's on you to cut them loose or keep dealing with flaky friends.

Lesson: A true friend feels like family. You love and encourage one another. You don't have to put up fronts or pretend. A true friend will push you to be the best person you can be by always encouraging and giving you the real deal about yourself. When you're with a true friend you will feel totally comfortable.

"Stick to your values."

Don't try to bend
or sway
I stand still
in my truth
I look for answers
within myself
I have the power of God
within this body
your words cannot move me
unless they speak pure truth
that which is right for me
Don't try to bend
or sway me
I can listen
but I will not change
unless it is in my destiny
leave your foolish thoughts
and attempts to manipulate
right there
I am a partner with God
I can hear
I can feel
I can see
when you are not right
for me

I know when you are trying to persuade me
to do what's right for you
and wrong for me
Don't try to bend
or sway me
I am too powerful for this
I know myself
and I am in love
with me
therefore I do what's right
for Me

At every moment you know what is right for you. It's just easy to get caught up in a moment and forget. You have to make sure that no man talks you out of or into any situation you don't want to be in. You have to realize the motivation behind other people's actions. Not everyone is looking out for your best interests. So what you have to do is remember that this is your world. There is no one in this world better than you. There is no one that knows you better than you. Therefore you're in control. You decide what is and is not acceptable. You make sure that the values your parents instilled do not get diminished.

Lesson: Your values are your life guide. They will help you make the right choices, if you listen. Always remember what you want out of life. Accept no imitations and go for it.

Taking Responsibility

Don't sit comfortably
thinking you know everything
life has twists and turns
that you must be prepared for
before you do
think of where
this will leave you
years from now

Every simple decision will have profound impact on your life. This means that everything you decide to do with your life will effect the outcome of your life. You have to think before you make choices. Don't decide on impulse. Know when to separate the emotions from the facts and make a decision based on facts. Many times as women we want to think with our hearts. But our hearts and our inner voices are not always on the same page. Your heart will keep you in some crazy situations. Your inner voice will always let you know when you need to get up and out.

Don't ever assume that someone else will be there for you to cover your responsibilities. This is your life. Every decision you make will affect your life. It will become your responsibility. People will be there for you but don't expect more from them than you expect or can give yourself.

Always think realistically. The worse mistake is to get caught up in the moment. You have to know when to step back and think. You always have to think for your best interests.

Life is not meant to be a series of challenges that leave you feeling defeated. It is, however, meant to shape your character. I remember people always telling me "God never gives us more than we can handle." At the time I thought, well, maybe he doesn't know me that well. It's easy to think that when times are really hard. But you can't give up. You have to look at the role you played in shaping your life. I advise you to look at your life and think before you make any choices or decisions. Think, because your life depends on it.

Lesson: The decisions we make each and every day will define what we have to be responsible for. Therefore we have to think before we make any choices or decisions about the impact we will be making on our lives.

Opening up to love after being hurt

Experience strengthens the soul
but does it harden the love
does betrayal
turn you inside yourself
until you run through
your own
mind
in search of truth
honesty
and hope
where does the love go
when experience
has hardened your innocent soul
and makes you untrusting of others
suspicious of all

The worst thing you can do is to keep yourself in a cycle of relationships. You have to take a breather between relationships. That time is necessary to let go of any anger and release the baggage. No one, besides a therapist, wants to deal with you and your problems.

If a relationship even has a tinge of "I'll get you through this," it will become fatal because the relationship will become needy. He'll need to help you, you'll need to be helped, you'll hurt him with your words and actions, he'll stick it through because "he loves you," he'll start hurting you, you'll stick with him because "you love him." It becomes one vicious mess that you could have avoided.

If a man has hurt you in any way in a prior relationship, do not immediately enter another relationship. Do not even begin to fool yourself and say it's just sexual. That's just a relationship diversion. You have to deal with yourself before you can give yourself, in any capacity, to anyone.

You have to know why and what you want from a relationship. Don't try to replace the last man with a new man. Don't try to hurt anyone because you've been hurt. Don't become bitter because the last man was a jerk. Because what you perceive will become your reality. If from your experiences you think all men are jerks and ain't about nothing, guess what type of men you're going to meet. Your perception is your reality.

You are fully empowered to take a break between relationships. It's like a breath of fresh air for your spirit. You get in tune with yourself and you don't become jaded, disillusioned or embittered. This is not to say that all relationships end badly and you need time to heal. Even if it was a good relationship you still need to take time to yourself. Comparing your man to your ex is just as bad as being bitter; it will ruin the relationship eventually. So always take time for yourself before dating or entering new relationships.

Once you have allowed yourself to heal, you're no longer thinking about your ex or comparing men to him, then you can consider dating. But always go into a relationship fresh. Leave behind the baggage and don't expect him to be a jerk or dog.

Expect the best treatment. Expect the best relationship. Don't become intimate immediately and don't start thinking this is the one. Get to know the man you're dealing with. Get to know him as your friend. Learn how to trust. Learn how to love. But do it slowly. Don't rush. A solid relationship needs a foundation of friendship, trust, respect, honesty and love. It takes time to create those qualities in one another.

You can open yourself up to love but know that love is reciprocal. You will love him and he will love you. You will not need one another. You will want one another. Love is not needy. Love is not possessive. Love is something that makes your life better and makes you feel happy.

Lesson: Between each relationship take a breather and renew your spirit. It will empower you to make better choices in relationships and give you time to know yourself.

"Learn from your experiences."

A simple message
in the bottle of your soul
is opened and revealed
by anyone around you
be aware
hear the words
learn what you must
and move on
but always know
that these lessons
are the fabric of your soul
and must be returned to you
one
by precious
one
to make you whole

A sign of wisdom is being able to look back on an experience and find the lesson. Life is all about learning and experiencing. You may not initially have the life you dreamed of. There may be some obstacles in the way, some experiences that hurt you and bring you down. The way you react to your experiences will be the deciding factor in how you will continue to live your life.

The *Tao Te Ching*, a spiritual book I highly recommend that you read, states that when life becomes difficult, the weak man falls down on himself and bewails his fate. The strong man sees it as an obstacle, a learning experience, and perseveres. Life is not about giving into your experiences and just saying this is it, this is all I will become.

You have to always remain in control of your life. By learning your lesson in every situation you are maintaining control of your life.

Lessons are everywhere in your life. You have to open your eyes and see them. When you're in the middle of a situation, you will not see the lesson. You will wonder *why me?* But you have to, for the sake of your sanity and the advancement of your life, stand back from the situation and see what's up. What was this situation supposed to teach you? Whether good or bad, there is a lesson. Also remember, that everything happens for a reason. Yes, everything. So look at your life, see the patterns, learn from your past decisions and make better choices in the future.

If you do not look for the lesson in your situations, you will be closing your eyes to your life. You will no longer be in power to change your life. You don't have to make the same mistakes. You don't have to be stuck in any situation. You just have to be willing to learn from your mistakes. If you are wise enough, you will look at the mistakes your friends have made and learn from their decisions as well.

If you choose not to learn your lesson the first time, it will be repeated. Don't think it won't.

Life is about going to the next level in every endeavor. Learn from your life and make it an example to others. God gave you this life and the chance to learn. This process, of learning lessons, is for the evolution of your spirit. You do not want to repeat lessons because your spirit wants and needs to continuously learn more. You have to push yourself to the next level. Control your destiny and your spiritual evolution.

Lesson: There are lessons in life we all must learn. The way we control our life is by opening our eyes to the lessons and making the right choices.

"Be open to opportunities."

If I close my eyes
because I don't want to see
but only welcome the darkness
is that a sanctuary?

If I open my eyes
and swallow the fear
follow through
even on shaky legs
does that make me courageous?

Though I may walk
with tears in my eyes
because I am afraid
of where the path leads
am I not brave
for at least walking?

If I say There
There is my destiny
and I stand still
and point
aren't I a fool?

The art
of the game
is embracing the fear
tucking the doubt
under your arm
running
and willing your way
to personal freedom

Don't limit your life to what others around you have achieved. Look at life as something that you can create. Explore life. Don't limit yourself to one thing. Learn new things. Look for the opportunities to learn and do new things. Never get caught up in the same day-to-day stuff. Life is not about redundancy. It is about pushing yourself to the next level and learning more about yourself. Every situation has the opportunity to teach you something about yourself and others. It's on you to put yourself in the position to learn. You have to extend yourself and reach into life.

Every person who is caught up in the day-to-day drama or not loving life is afraid of risk. In this life you have to take risks to push yourself to the next level and get more out of life. You have to always want more. Not materialistically, but to always learn. If you are not taking risks, you are not living life.

Lesson: Life is full of opportunities. You have to embrace them and allow the fear to push you forward. This is your life to create.

"Do not give up on yourself."

In your lowest moment
at your hardest time
you are being created
your will being tested
your spirit struggling

if you allow it
and open your heart
to the lesson
your true spirit will emerge
your soul will be the guide
in your life
and you will find that God never left you
she was only giving you a mirror
into your inner soul
to find how you will define your life
and whether your experiences will make
or break you.

The lesson in life is that
God is always with you,
within you
in your heart
and the way you express yourself

God is your soul.
Your soul is part of God.
Once you know this fully and completely
you can create the life you want
and handle any adversity.

We can be our own worst critic. When something goes wrong in our life it is easy to put ourselves down and condemn ourselves as a failure. You're never a failure if you are trying. What you have to do is recognize the mistakes you have made and learn from them. This will help you to make better decisions in the future.

Once you have learned that you will make mistakes and can learn from them, you have no reason to ever give up on yourself. This is your life and at any moment you have the opportunity to make it what you want.

Giving up on yourself hurts your spirit. It can cause stress, depression, anxiety and doubts. It can hinder you from exploring new opportunities. It can allow you to stay in terrible situations and accept things you never should. Don't ever do this to yourself. You always are in control. You just have to say, okay, this didn't work, now what can I do?

Stay in control of your life. Stress and giving up on yourself will kill you, literally and spiritually.

Always know that you can have more out of life. You don't have to limit yourself. You don't have to be afraid. You can achieve what you want.

You are not a failure. You are human and we will all have failures and mistakes. You just have to get up and keep going. Keep living life.

Lesson: Giving up on yourself kills your spirit and can make your life become stagnant.

"Know your definition of success."

If I have
If I have
If I have
everything
except you
I have nothing
You are my love
my world
I want to share this
with you
I need to have you
You are what I want
in my life
you make all this complete
then it's real
then there's happiness
then I have everything

Success is an inner fulfillment. It is not money or a beautiful home. You will be at a level of success when you are constantly learning and growing, allowing yourself to be open to love and sharing that love. Success is not about status. It is about reaching a goal.

It is best to know early in life what your definition of success is. It varies for many. For many people a certain income level defines their success. You have to be deeper than that. Money allows you to do the things that will make you happy. But you should not love money. Money is a materialistic means to an end. Never focus your love on money. Focus on the opportunities you can have and give to others through money.

Don't define success as a beautiful home or car. These are also materialistic things. They are not permanent fixtures. If you allow them to define who you are your definition will be shallow. You have to look beyond what a car says about you and get a car because you like it. The same thing is true with your choice in a home, it is a reflection of you, but it does not define who you are. You define who you are and therefore define what success is.

Success is not a permanent state. All your life you must seek to learn and acquire new goals. Always push your "success" to the next level.

Lesson: Success is an inner fulfillment. It is not based on material or physical items. It is about reaching a level of comfort where you love yourself and are happy with yourself.

"Live in Love"

Healing a Broken Heart

Love is the food
of your soul
never give up on it
you need it
for your spirit to breathe

You can get through this. I know it feels so painful, as though your heart's been pulled out of your mouth. But you have to tell yourself, I can get through this. Repeat it as often as you need it. Say it until you believe it. I can get through this.

When love ends, we can feel confused and hurt. We feel as if we'll never love again, like *the one* just got away. But true love does not get away from you. True love is there when you need it, when you are ready for it. So realize that although you loved this person, you have to let them go, so your true love can enter.

Don't do foolish things while you're in pain. Don't try to make him hurt the way he hurt you. Just let it go. I know it sounds simple. I know your heart is in pain, but if you want to deal with this you're going to have to think realistically. You're going to have to listen to the reasons the relationship ended. You're going to have to think about your part in the breakup. Analyze the relationship. See what lesson you can learn from it.

Even when I felt like my heart was breaking I stopped and said, I was supposed to learn this. He was supposed to teach me this. No it didn't make me feel that much better. But I learned my lesson and that was the ultimate point.

Everything happens for a reason. If a relationship ends, let it end. Sometimes fighting is just delaying the inevitable. Sometimes you will just bring yourself more pain if you don't let go at the right time. Know when to take a breath and let go.

Lesson: You can mend your heart. You can get through any pain. Just relax, feel the hurt, take as much time as you need to get over it. You can get through this and things will get better if you learn your lesson and apply it in the next relationship.

"Show people that you appreciate them."

When you say thank you
it makes me smile
I know then
that you realize
that I took my time
invested my energy
in you
you know
to get some more
of me
you always have to say
thank you for that
I appreciate it

It is very easy to take others for granted. We get used to them being a part of our lives and doing things for us. We have to know that people are in our lives because they choose to be. They do things for us because that is their choice. Even your parents have a choice in how much they will do for you. You have to remember that everyone in your life who does things for you should be appreciated.

Say thank you when things are done for you. Even in life when it seems that things are coincidentally working out for you, say thank you to God. There is always someone or something working for your best good. The more open you are to saying thank you and appreciating the time and energy others give to you, the more you will receive out of life.

Appreciation is a form of reciprocal love. When you can appreciate the people and events in your life you will notice that life goes more smoothly. You will realize the beauty in the world and within others.

Showing your appreciation is a simple act that you can perform everyday that will greatly affect your life and the lives of others.

Lesson: Showing your appreciation to and for others will greatly affect your outlook on life.

"Treat others as you would want to be treated."

Queen

or king

Peasant

or pawn

treat me

as you would want to be regarded

because whether I do it or not

it will come back to you

when you least expect it

and break you down

or lift you up

Now this sounds like something we all would believe. However, if you keep it real with yourself you don't always treat others as you would want to be treated. We get caught up in our day, our mood, ourselves and can take that out on others. It's easy to spread your cheer when you're in a good mood, but when you're in a bad mood are you spreading that too?

We have to be mindful of the feelings of others. If we took just one moment and thought of the other person this would be a much better world. Consideration goes a long way in the scheme of things.

If you take the moment to think of the feelings of another person before you react, you will shape that experience. You have the power to control your day by how you respond and treat others.

If you treat others as you would want to be treated you will be rewarded. You'll be rewarded with better relationships, friendships and basically a better life.

Lesson: Treat others as you would want to be treated and you will be rewarded with better relationships.

Abusive Relationships

Always wondered
how a woman could say
my man loves me
when she doesn't know where he goes
at night
always wondered
how love could be believed
when people are sneaking
and deceiving
always wondered
how things were right
as long as he was there
to pay the bills
is it all right to be smacked
long as he sticks around
and pays the rent
I'm wondering when it became alright
to receive black eyes
and be dragged
by the throat
are these loving hands
the father of your child
green keeps these people together
green love for one another

I'm wondering when you became dependent
on men who beat you
cheat on you
and lie to you
many a person has said
you are worth more
wondering if there are marbles in your head
I want to scream out loud
when I see you
no longer covering those eyes
raccoon style is now your badge
of honor
where is life headed
when you no longer feel ashamed
signs of love do not beat your side
pain your heart
or make you cry all night
I'm wondering why
it hurts me
more than
it seems to hurt you

In a perfect world I would not even have to mention someone being abused mentally or physically. But there are women every day getting beat down and staying in the relationship.

I have to emphasize to you that the way you think about yourself directly affects what you will expect and receive in relationships. On the surface you may appear to have it all together, but only women with insecurities and low self-esteem stay in these situations, and if they're trying to rationalize it, they're just all-out stupid.

If a man hits you even once, he will hit you again. Never let any man think he can get away with that. Yes, he may have more strength than you but everyone has to sleep.

It's really painful to see a woman put herself through this torture. There is nothing that should keep anyone in this type of relationship. Don't second guess yourself. It's not worth staying to 'keep the family together' or because of finances. You will eventually end up without a shred of self-esteem and will take years to rebuild yourself. It's simply not worth it.

There is always someone to turn to, some place to go.

I have never been in this type of relationship and never will, but I have seen it firsthand. I have seen how a grown woman can feel like a child in her own home, afraid to speak, afraid to leave her room. I have seen the scars and the tears. I have seen the damage done in a room of "love" after a man has beaten a woman. I have heard what it sounds like. It's worse than any nightmare. It's hell.

Don't put yourself in this situation. There are always early warning signs. You can detect when a brother is a little too possessive. It is not even remotely cute for a brother to want to know where you are every minute of the day. It's none of his business. Realize that a brother trying to change the way you dress or pick out your clothes is trying to change you. He is trying to mold you into what he wants. You cannot allow this to happen. Stay true to you.

I would strongly caution against being with someone who said he had beaten a girlfriend who pushed him to it in the past. That's not acceptable. This brother has no control over his emotions and will simply pull you into his world with his irrationality. Don't even finish the conversation. Get out of there and never look back.

Now, there are also brothers that will not hit, but will put you down with words. They are attempting to break your spirit because they themselves have no strength, no inner spirit. You must never allow anyone to disrespect you in any way. This even happens in marriages because the woman believes that the husband knows her well. There is not a man in this world that knows you well enough to cut you down to shreds. Any man that tries to rationalize his disrespect towards you is a waste of your life and your time. Don't listen to his crap. Initially, you may waive it off but it will stick in your mind and you will come to believe his negative words. Get out while you are sane enough to know that you are a beautiful, intelligent woman who deserves the world.

Lesson: Never allow anyone to abuse you in any way. They will kill you, either literally or spiritually.

When to end a friendship

Childhood dreams are my memories
you and I faithful friends
ever alike
now where we stand as adults
is on two different sides
you are my friend of yesteryears
a child
still exploring life with wonder
though not as a student of life
ignorance is your teacher, your friend
knowledge is my guide
how can we remain friends
on two different sides
I know you so well
you know me not at all
you stand in front of me a child
and I do not understand
I do not understand

As with everything in life, there are signs. There are beginnings and there are endings. Sometimes friends grow apart. They know longer have anything in common and the relationship feels strained. You have to know when to end a relationship of any kind, particularly when you are not growing in the relationship or are no longer enjoying the person's company.

You can feel when you are growing apart from people. You just tolerate them because you have known them for so long. You listen to what they're saying halfway. But you know you're not interested in what they're saying. Essentially you're know longer interested in their life.

It's a hard decision, but you have to know when to say this is it. You may not want to hurt their feelings, especially if you've known them since grade school or something, but you're stifling your life. When you allow yourself to listen to their conversations and go places with them you don't really want to go, you are wasting your time and therefore stifling and limiting your life, you could be out doing things you enjoy. Instead you're putting yourself through needless motions.

You may not want to come right out and say "this friendship is no longer working." It is the best thing to do. You may just want to phase out their phone calls. You may stop going out with them, but if they consider you a friend they're going to want to know why you're distancing yourself from them. The best thing you can do, initially then, is put an end to this relationship that is wasting your time. You will have to be mature and keep it real with the girl. Cut her loose and live your life. Don't try to mend something that's broken.

When you're young, you think you'll be friends with your high school friends forever. And some of them you will stay friends with. But many you will outgrow. The best thing is to acknowledge this and move on. There are so many people in this world that you do not have to limit yourself or go through the motions just to make someone else happy.

Lesson: A progressive life is one in which you know when to end relationships that are hindering your spiritual and intellectual growth.

"Go for your highest goal."

You will never have true happiness
until you do what fulfills you

Somewhere within your spirit there is something that you really want to do in this life. There is something you want to accomplish more than anything else. Sometimes, however, when you share that dream, you can be put down. People will tell you to be realistic, and you will push your dream to the side. I'm telling you now, don't even think of curbing your dream.

Reality is what you make it. Whatever you choose to do in this life, whatever you pursue wholeheartedly, you will achieve. You simply have to be willing to believe that it is yours to achieve. You have to know that you are meant to have that lifestyle that will come with achieving your dream. You have to push away the negative thoughts and "realistic advice" people are pushing on you and keep moving towards your dream.

People waste more than a little bit of time in life listening to the opinions of others. No one can tell you what to want in your life. No one can define your dream. Anything you feel that strongly is your purpose in your life. That means you have to fulfill that dream in order to live a life you love.

We all know what we want out of this life. We are just often disillusioned into thinking we can not achieve it. You have to tune out the voices of others, listen to your heart and work at making your highest goal your reality. If you believe it, if you want it, and are willing to work for it, you can and will achieve your goals. It just depends on how badly you want to achieve that dream. If your desire is strong, there is nothing, and no one, that can deter you from achieving your dream.

Lesson: The dream that you really want is what will help you achieve your spiritual purpose in life. That is the reason you are here on this earth, so you have to work towards it and live a life you love.

"Your expectations determine your reality."

What you wish
is what you get
what you want
is what you see
train your mind
live through the third eye
and visualize life
as you want it
focus on that
you will see
dreams can
become reality

You know what you're doing when you say, I can't do this. You are limiting your life. That means whatever you repeat to yourself your mind will interpret as reality. Therefore your saying you cannot do this or that becomes true to your mind. Then you've limited your capabilities by thinking a foolish thought.

You have to program your mind to know that you can achieve what you want, you can have what you want, you can have a life you love. How do you program your mind? You tell yourself all the things you need to hear to push yourself forward. Everything that you wish someone would say to inspire you, say to yourself. If you need to hear that you're beautiful in order to feel confident, tell yourself you're beautiful.

Be your own inspiration. You do not have to look for outside inspiration or heroes. You can do these things yourself. You can look up to others but they're not going to make you feel good about yourself. Only you can do that through your thinking and what you make your reality.

The reason you need to program your mind is so that you will have a strong foundation. In this life you have to have self-confidence, self-esteem, ambition, and be determined. The only way you can possess those qualities though is to internally and fully believe that you are the best. If you keep telling yourself terrible things such as "I can't, I won't, I never" you will doom your life to those realities. If you want to have a life in which you are happy you have to gear yourself to the upside of the life. The *I can achieve whatever I want, there's no one in this world better than me, I can live a life I love* type of thinking.

Think of the life you want. Focus on those things. Because whatever you focus on you will achieve.

Lesson: Life is what you expect to happen. Your perception and belief system will affect what you experience and what you achieve in this life.

"Shape your life"

"Who or what is God?"

If you don't know
you have no foundation
without that
you cannot build
you cannot feel
you cannot experience
you have to find the love
that exists within you
the love that others have
for you
and realize
that is just a glimpse
of the love of the universe
the embrace of God

God is a spiritual being that exists within you, within others and within the world. God is a force that created you and everything in this world. God created the world as a place for man and nature to coincide.

God is not a wrathful, vengeful being. He or She is not someone you should have fear of. There is no reason at all to be a God-fearing person. God created everything in nature to work with and complement one another. The sunsets, the mountains, the earth itself, are things of beauty. A being that created all these wonderful things is not something you fear. You can be awe of the works of God, but to be fearful of God is absurd. God is a loving being that you should love.

In the same way that nature complements itself, humans are also here to complement one another. That means that life is about learning and about giving. All you have to do in this life is learn about yourself and give what you know. Life is really not difficult if you look at it in those simple terms God has given us.

You learn in this life through your experiences. Those experiences shape your life, your character, your values, your belief, your goals, your love, your reality. While you are going through your life lessons you will have a goal you want to fulfill. This goal is your reason for being. Because while you are here to learn, you are also here to fulfill a purpose. Fulfilling that purpose is like completing an agreement with God. He gave you a desire and you have to achieve it.

When you fulfill that dream, your spiritual purpose, you are giving the most beautiful thing to the world. You are giving yourself as a completely fulfilled person. This is the reason you are here: to learn, to give, to fulfill your purpose.

Your purpose is what you most desire. Any ambition, any goal is acceptable, whether it's to start a daycare center or become an entertainment lawyer. The outcome is still the same; you will be in a position to help others.

To always remember your purpose, you have to remember that God is within you. Since God is the creator, you are in some way co-creator of your life. You can create the life you want by simply believing you should achieve it. Whatever you focus on and work towards, you will achieve.

Fulfilling your purpose is a spiritual act. There is not a way to tune into your spirituality. It is about looking within and looking at the world. This world is beautiful, you will see that if you look. It's easy to look at the negative things and the bitter people and think this world is ugly. But the world becomes ugly because people don't realize that they are creators of their life. There is no one who has to remain miserable or unhappy. That's a choice.

Really look at the world, the trees, the oceans, the mountains. All of it is beautiful and designed with a specific purpose. They all automatically work well together. Your responsibility is to fulfill your purpose so that in some way you make the world work well.

One person can make a difference and that is what you are here to do. If you touch the life of one person you are creating a domino effect. That person will touch the life of another person and so on. So always know that your fulfilling your dream is a necessity.

Lesson: God is not to be feared. He is to be loved. God is within you and therefore you have the power to create the life you want. When you create the life you want, that inner fulfillment and happiness, will be passed on to others as an inspiration.

First Sex

Did you ever love someone
so much
that it felt like a dream
just too good to be true
but so strong you can't deny

You want to show him
that you love him
you appreciate him
you adore him

in every way
A love that makes you feel all aglow
just by
the thought of him

His words are gold
like nectar to your soul
inspiring you
touching you
in just the right way

A love that seems like a gift
because no one can be better than this
and you know that he loves you
in the same beautiful way

Sex should always be with someone you love. You never want to do anything you'll regret. You also don't want to do it because you got caught up in the moment or just to get it out of the way. Your first sexual experience is going to define how you feel about being intimate for the rest of your life. You better make sure you know what love is and that this is a person you love.

Although I'm not that much older than you, our worlds are sometimes completely different. In my day, I know that sounds old, but really, in my day it was an honor to be a virgin. You felt devastated and disgusted if anyone tried to say you weren't a virgin. You did not want to be accused of having sex at such an early age.

Now though, you girls are acting as if being a virgin is like being called a slut. You have your morals backwards. Stay a virgin until you find a man you love. Emphasis on man. Young boys often only want one thing.

It's a rarity for every woman to find a guy that treats her like gold and honors her. But that's the one you want. You want a guy that is going to appreciate that he's your first. Not because he's glad to get some. But because he really loves you and is glad you're sharing such an intimate experience with him.

I do not regret my first sexual experience. I was old enough to know I wanted to be with him and mature enough to know that this guy loved me. We still love and respect one another. That's what you want to be able to say. So choose who you want to be with wisely.

If you do decide to have sex please use protection. You can wind up a young unhappy mother or a young woman with AIDS. I know a girl who was diagnosed as HIV positive her first semester of college. She had only been sleeping with one guy. She still looks "normal." So don't assume any stupid crap, like you'd be able to tell. You won't know until a doctor diagnoses you, so use protection.

Also, if you're going to have sex, make sure you have a loving environment. I can't believe the number of women that have lost their virginity in the backseat of cars. I personally just think that's disgusting, degrading and unacceptable. There's no love in the backseat of a car. That's a quickie. Keep it real with yourself and make sure, again, that this is a person that loves and respects you. No man that respects or loves you would even consider having you lose your virginity in those demeaning ways.

You have to be sure you both want to take this relationship to another level. Sex is just another extension of a relationship. Never have sex because you think it will make a relationship better. Or the most idiotic thing I've heard, "because everyone else is doing it."

If you're not able to talk to your parents about protection, as many young girls aren't, see if there is someone else you can talk to about it. It's a lot easier to ask for protection now then to go through an unwanted pregnancy or receive a terrible disease. So ask an aunt or family friend or walk your butt into the closest Planned Parenthood center.

Don't expect the stuff you see on tv. First sex is usually nothing like that, even when it's with someone you love. You'll both be a little nervous and will not really know what you're doing.

I don't think you should have sex when you're so young because it can add complications to your life. Plus sex is much better when you're mature and know the difference between love and infatuation. However, being realistic, I know there are many girls who are just as willing as boys to take it to another level. So just remember to share yourself with someone you genuinely love and always use protection.

Lesson: Sex is an intimate act between a couple that loves and respects one another.

"Don't spread your misery."

Words
can come back
so watch
what you throw out
a little fake pms here
can win you
b of the year
lonely & miserable
with no one to shed a tear with
watch what you throw out
say what you feel
a stack of apologies
are nothing but garbage
to the pain caused a soul
by your insensitive
foolish remarks
watch your bitterness
before it spreads
through your body
and manifests as
experience
nothing but lies
because you'd rather hide your heart
and let your mouth flow

that misery is reeking girl
pretty soon
everyone will
run from you

There are many females that treat their men like crap. They yell at them and put them down. I have a friend that yelled at her man so bad in front of me it sent chills down my spine. If a man irritates you that much, then you should strongly consider being single. Why would you be with someone that you obviously don't respect and cannot love? If you love someone, then you care about his feelings. You care about how your words will affect him.

There's a misconception that in order to have a strong relationship you have to have your man in check, that what you say goes. Now there's nothing wrong with having some control in a relationship. You don't want to be passive. But you also want to make sure that the control of the relationship is in both of your hands.

Imagine someone yelling at you, even in front of your friends, and telling you what to do and when to do it. You'd kick him to the curb with a quickness. Yet instead we expect the men in our lives to take our drama, our yelling and screaming as female tendencies, when really we need to consider their feelings as well as we would consider ours. No, they are not as emotional as we are. Yes, they can take the yelling a little bit better than we can. But do they want to deal with this stuff? Oh hell no, they don't. They deal with it until they can no longer take it anymore. So watch what you yell and get so upset about that you don't tell your man he's stupid and whatever else comes to your mind.

A true lady treats her man with the same respect she would want. A woman knows that she doesn't have to put anyone down in order to make herself feel better.

Keep your expectations of your man realistic. If he didn't do something before marriage he's not suddenly going to do it when he's married. You have to look at the person you're with for the person he is right now. Realize that the things you determine as important or essential may not be so important to your man. No one wants to hear you nag and yell. Your friends don't even want to hear about how you had to nag him. It's all just too irritating and eventually you want to get away from that nagging, miserable person as soon as you can.

Lesson: Realize that what you deem to be important and essential may not be as important to others. This does not lessen the importance. It just means that you realize the situation will be reversed. Whatever your friend or man finds important or essential, you may not think is so important. But you still respect one another and the right you each have to determine when, what and how you want to do things in your life.

"Confidence is not an attitude. It's a state of mind."

confidence is not an attitude
it is knowing
feeling
believing
confidence is an assertion
a proclamation
I am the best
because I am me

I know when you see people you believe are confident, you look at the way they walk, their face, their words. But confidence is not an attitude. It's a state of mind. There are many people out there walking the confidence walk that are really very insecure.

So while you do want to have your confident walk and look as if you have your stuff together, you also want to really have your stuff together. That means believing in yourself, loving yourself, respecting yourself.

How do you believe in yourself? Your beliefs have been affected by many things in your life. Your parents, your friends, television, your family, your boyfriends, all have had a part in shaping your belief system. Whatever they have instilled in your mind has become your reality, your truth. If they are positive things such as you're beautiful, you're intelligent, you can be anything you want, you are loved, then hold onto those beliefs.

If however you've had a much harsher glimpse of life and people and even your parents have put you down then you have to let all of that go and rebuild yourself. You have to realize that what anyone says about you does not matter. It will only affect you for as much or as long as you allow it. Often people put others down because they can't see life the way you do. Their life has become closed. When people hurt you it may not always be intentional. It may just be the only way they know how to relate. But these are their personal problems that you cannot allow to affect you any longer.

So to believe in yourself you have to have a foundation of love, respect, and confidence within and for yourself. You have to eliminate any negative beliefs you have and live life in a more loving way.

To love yourself, you have to like yourself. You have to like the person you are. The person you are is shaped by the decisions you have made and what you believe. When you make any decision, you have to base that on whether the decision is truly a reflection of you. When you make decisions that are a reflection of who you really are, and live your life based on your truth, you become a person that you can respect and love.

Lesson: Confidence is an essential state of being. It is based on loving, respecting and appreciating yourself. Make decisions based on who you are and want to be as a person. This will help you like and love yourself, which will give you more confidence.

Dealing with death

Angels of light
shining brightly
warming the soul
through memories
pictures of love
you are my angel now
I love you more
than I could ever say
I feel your spirit
and I thank you
for sticking with me
in this time of need
by showing me
that heaven is having peace
and sharing it
I see you every night
in the stars
I see you in the stream of light
cascading from the sun
I see you in the mirror
when I smile
I know as long as I have love for you
I have you
You are my angel
I love you

Somehow we expect you to be able to deal with death even though we ourselves cannot. As though you didn't love as much as we did. Or that you simply don't understand the magnitude of the situation. But I know you understand. I know you're hurting.

Death is a continuation, not an end. That means that when someone close to you dies, they simply go somewhere else. Though they have left your physical world and you can't see them, they still exist. They exist in your heart and your memories. They exist in heaven. Their spirit is with God.

It's devastating as a young person to deal with death. While you don't question your own immortality, you don't think you're going to die tomorrow, you do wonder if everyone around you is going to start dying. It's very scary and traumatic. Realistically, everyone is going to die. And I think parents and loved ones try to hide that fact from you. It's not fair and it doesn't make dealing with death any easier. If anything, you just think they're in denial.

Everyone does eventually pass on to be with God once again. So what you can do now is focus on the time you have with people. Live life to the fullest. Let people know you love and care about them. And always know that if someone is sick or in need you should be there for them. It's important to you and it's important to that person.

One day, my dear, you are going to pass on too. That does not mean that you give in to grief and stress and take your own life. Your life is a precious gift. You have a spiritual agreement with God to live, learn and love here. If you are in need of someone to get you through a tough time then reach out and ask for that help. Don't think there's no one to help or to listen. There are many people that are very loving and willing to help.

It is painful to lose someone you love. It's hard to deal with, but remember they live on not only in your heart but their spirit is still present, still looking over you. Now you have your own personal angel.

Lesson: Realize that death is something that will happen to everyone. Therefore you should tell and show people that you love and appreciate them. You should also live your life completely in a way that you will enjoy and have no regrets.

"Have goals."

One, Two, Three, Go
Go
Go where
you didn't know
you better find out
Oh My God
can we start again
you crazy
you better keep running
But where am I going
You should have known that
before you left the gate
Run girl
Run

The thing many women regret is that they didn't make wise choices with their lives. They feel as though they just got caught up in life, simply taking whatever job was available, dating whatever man asked them out. It doesn't mean they were taking crap, just that they allowed life to lead them. If there's anything women would change in life, it's their focus. Honestly, they would have paid more attention to their education and less to the boyfriend they thought they loved to death.

It's necessary for your happiness to know what you want out of life. High school can be fun and one of the best times of your life. But when you graduate life is going to come at you head on and you're going to have to know how to deal. Knowing, as they say, is half the battle. Once you know don't let anything or anyone deter you. You will come to regret it if you do. Make decisions that are right for you.

I'm going to go all out for you and admit mama is not always right. There are many mothers and daughters that are not emotionally close, and therefore mama telling you what to do is not as accurate as a friend who truly knows you. Yes mama wants the best for you, but if she doesn't know you know you, she can be misleading you. You'll know deep down what's right for you.

The next step is to make a life plan. Because once you know what you want out of life, you have to plan ways and deadlines to achieve it. Life will be so much easier for you this way. So write down your goals and write down what you need to do to accomplish them. Then make your choices based on achieving those goals. Intern in your field. Take entry-level jobs in that area. Don't think any job is unimportant. Every job is important when you have a life plan. When you have a life plan, the jobs you choose are going to be based on getting you closer to your dream. That means instead of being a fry cook, you'll be a receptionist so you'll learn how to deal with clients. Use your jobs to your advantage and don't get comfortable. That's another trap.

There are many people that started jobs at young ages and never left. That's your parents generation. For many, once they got a good job they stayed put. Now however that situation is no longer a reality. And it's not something you need to make your reality anyway. You're not at a job to make friends. You're there to learn and grow. You want to have a job that challenges and pushes you towards your goals. Don't ever get complacent and just try to stick it out. If it's not your dream job, it's just a step along the way. Definitely don't quit one job until you have another. But always keep learning new things and looking for opportunities to get closer to your goals.

Learn from the mistakes of other women. Take control of your life. Make a life plan and stick to it. Accomplish your goals. Yes, you can work toward your goals at any age. But it's so much easier when you haven't become stagnant, complacent, you don't have overwhelming responsibilities and you can simply live your life.

Lesson: Take control of your life by making a life plan, a listing of your goals, and ways to accomplish them.

"Use your resources"

"Don't tell too much about your man."

If you keep saying
something is sooo good
pretty soon
someone will want to know
if it's better than what they got
and just how good
is sooo good

When we enter a relationship that is thrilling us, we feel joyful and want to share that experience. We want to tell our friends and family just how wonderful this man is. We want them to know how special and loved he makes us feel. But as many Black women say "A good man is hard to come by" and if you keep talking about yours, while they're dealing with crap, they're going to either get jealous, distant, or want what you've got.

Every woman wants to be treated special, with respect and love. But not everyone can deal with how wonderful your relationship is if they're not currently experiencing the same thing. It is in your best interest to just hold back with the info sometimes. No one needs to know what goes on in the bedroom or what he says to you to make you feel so special.

Also be careful of having your best friend and your man around one another all the time. Of course you want to spend time with both, but they may become cozier than you'd like.

Remember that your friends and family do want you to be happy. But to remain happy, you have to keep some of your business to yourself.

Lesson: The best relationship is one in which the partners honor the commitment and sacredness of their relationship.

"Kick Mr. Potential to the curb."

When you try to pull
someone up
they can pull you down
if their will to stay
is stronger
than your desire
to rise

Kick Mr. Potential to the curb. Yes, that sounds harsh. But this Mr. Potential is the one you're saying would be a better man if ____. This is the man you like and could learn to love. This is the guy you think will someday be a decent man. This is a guy that has drama. He is a walking headache. This is not the brother that's busting his butt to make something of his life. Oh no, this Mr. Potential is the whining, complaining, lazy, brother "that just can't get a break." This brother is the one you run like the wind from.

Mr. Potential has had a couple of breaks in his life. He was just starting to do this when this happened. Or he was just about to make it and then bam somebody did that. Don't think life is going to get better for the brother now that you're here. Your friendship and/or love is not going to help this brother. The only person that can help him is himself. Mr. Potential has to create his own life. You can't try to make it for him. He has to get past the potential and learn how to be a man for himself, by himself.

This is one of those *do I want to be happy or do I want to survive?* moments. Life is more than survival. Go for the happiness and kick Mr. Potential with no ambition to the curb.

Lesson: You cannot (always) change the life of another with your good intentions or friendship. If someone wants to change their life they will have to want it for themselves.

"Don't put marriage before the relationship."

Going to the
what's his name
Please
I'm about to get
what's his mama's name
I got this ring
what does he do
I don't care
I got everything I need

Many women are so focused on an engagement ring and wedding day that they completely look past the faults of the man they're dealing with. Women seem to be under the false impression that a man will change when he gets married. If he's cheating on you now, if he doesn't cook or clean up after himself, if he doesn't help with the kids, if he doesn't like your family and they don't like him, guess what? Nothing's going to change. Except your focus will be off your beautiful wedding day and onto how unhappy you are with this brother that can't even wash a dish or pick up his clothes.

Initially in dating, men let you see a sweet, wonderful, considerate side of them. Then as they get more used to you they let their guard down. If they are in fact sweet, considerate guys they stay that way. If, however, they were just trying to make a good impression and now they're being real, take that realness as a sign of God and get out if you can't deal. If you can't deal with dirty dishes, a cluttered floor, and a brother that sits still while the kids cry, stop the relationship now. Marriage is nothing but a continuation of what you have now.

Another reason not to run around saying he's the one is because you have really got to know this brother. I don't care what he says. I don't care if he's describing your dream life. Don't start looking at white dresses. Make sure the brother is not just telling you what you want to hear or what he needs to hear. You have to realize that sometimes people are just talk. Look at his life.

See what he's doing to make his dreams reality. Do his actions describe him as a considerate, loving, ambitious man or does he tell you this is the type of person he is? Before you fall for anyone make sure that they have shown and proved that they are worthy of your love and your time.

Also, when you're not busy deciding what carat you want, you allow the relationship to unfold. You allow the relationship to take its own course. This is very important and very necessary. When the focus is off of "is he the one?" you can focus on the friendship within the relationship. You can honestly get to know the man. You're not overlooking any flaws. You're appreciating the things he does for you. You're building a relationship.

Lesson: Marriage is a continuation of a relationship. It should be experienced with someone you love and regard as a friend. Someone that you want to grow with and share your life with. Someone that you love with the very essence of your being. The only way to find out if a man is that someone is to give it time. Take your eyes off the carat and look at the man. Make sure he's the right fit for your life.

"Don't try to compensate for your man's hard-knock life."

You cannot be the crutch
if there is no will to stand
You cannot be the life
if there is no desire to live
You cannot be the love
if the heart is closed
You cannot be the dream maker
if there are no wishes to fulfill
You cannot be everything
You cannot be anything
to someone
who doesn't want
an uncomplicated life

There are so many talented, beautiful woman that get caught up in the drama of their man's life. If a man is experiencing drama when you meet him and you continue to date him, you're asking for trouble. If he's just getting over drama, you're asking for trouble. This is not to say that men have to go through things in life alone, but rather that women tend to try to compensate for their men.

Every sister that is struggling with a man, pretty much, will tell you he had a hard life. His family situation was terrible. They just didn't treat him right. They still don't treat him right. It's like he's not part of the family. You know what I say, boo hoo. This man, this relationship, will kill your spirit. Eventually you won't know where life went because the years have passed you by.

There is no amount of love or friendship that can make up for the traumas this brother has experienced. Your loving cannot substitute for the therapist and counselor the brother so desperately needs. You are not the owner of his problems. You should not try to be his one good friend or example of loving family. You are just pulling yourself into some avoidable drama.

You have to realize that no one has a perfect family life. And the amount of Black women that have dealt with or seen child abuse, domestic violence, infidelity, etc. is astronomical. But still we persevere. We get up everyday and go through life. We find jobs. We find rides. We find daycare. We find a way. A real man would do the same thing.

For your own peace of mind and a better life, allow this man to find his own strength. Allow him to find his way. And never try to compensate for the issues a brother has been dealing with for years. You will only hurt yourself and allow him to become dependent and needy of you.

This is a stifling, unhappy relationship that has no positive outcome. The only reality will be a miserable, struggling life.

Lesson: You cannot compensate for the hard life of another person by trying to be their everything. People need a chance to heal without having another person as a crutch.

"Don't judge or limit yourself by the thoughts of others."

While you have a right
to your opinions and such
I am the only one
who can define me
so your opinions
don't matter much

It's easy to fall into the trap and believe the things people say about us. It is easy to think, well, maybe they're right. But this line of thinking gives people power over your life. They are defining your life and what you will become. You never want to give anyone power over your life. You have to disregard whatever anyone says about you and believe in yourself.

Sometimes you have to literally stop yourself in your life and say *this is it.* This is my life. I define it. I live it. I control it. Then you have to make decisions for yourself. Wherever you focus your energy, you focus your time. You cannot waste mental energy or time focusing on what others think of you.

Even loved ones will try to tell you what to do with your life. You have to thank them for their opinion and make your own decision. No one who constantly allowed his or her life to be directed by others led a happy life.

Don't give in to the shapers of society. Don't think you have to be thin, you have to look a certain way, you have to wear a certain label. Be your own person. Be original. Love the way you are.

Lesson: Never allow others to define your life because then they will control you.

"Have children when you're ready, not because you love some man."

There is no love
better than this
the person
that kisses my soul
shares my dreams
wants a life
with me
this man I love
that loves me
does not rush me
as we fulfill our dreams
we will see
when the time is right
for our souls to meet
and bring that light
into the world

As women it is easy to feel that we are in love with or love a man. We feel that if he treats us right, respects us, is there with us, we can give him our all. Usually we can. But there are those instances when a woman didn't take enough time to get to know the man she was dealing with. Either she became intimate or she thought she was in love too early in the relationship.

Relationships need time to develop. And we cannot give in to our hearts so quickly that we don't know deep down if this is The One. I personally thought I had met a great person. He was loving and considerate. And then things changed. The relationship changed. And I was left in a situation I never expected. I was a single parent.

There is no amount of preparation that can help you with being a single parent. It is difficult. It is challenging. It will change your life.

If you don't want to be in this situation, then get to know the guy you're dealing with. Don't become intimate too soon because you feel you're in love. Wait until you really know this person. Know that you love him. Know that you want to spend the rest of your life with him. And that the feelings are reciprocated.

A friend gave me this topic to include in the book. When he first said it, it felt like a slap in the face. It was if he was saying, Tasha why didn't you think before you had children with this guy? And I felt terrible because I had thought I didn't just rush into a relationship. I didn't say this is the one. But I did allow those infatuation feelings to be misguided as love. I then had sex early in the relationship. And a cycle began, because I became pregnant and then I felt stuck. I wasn't supposed to be a single parent, so I felt intent on making the relationship work. I felt it was my obligation to give my children a family. My main motivation was making sure my daughters had their father in their lives.

The one thing I do remember though, is ignoring my intuition. I remember, so clearly now, my intuition saying, this isn't the one. I chose to ignore that little voice and continue with the relationship because he was a sweet guy. He was a sweet guy but he wasn't the one. And now I'm something I didn't want to be, a single parent.

My advice to you is to know the difference between love and infatuation. Know that this man is someone you can depend on. Know that he is someone that has dreams, goals and plans. Know that he has a decent relationship with his family. Know that he doesn't use drugs of any kind. Know what you are getting yourself into when you enter a relationship. Know that the relationship is as important to him as it is to you. Know him well. Then get to know him some more. Know that you love him fully and completely. Spend time with him, share life with him, until you know one another well.

Lesson: Make sure that you have taken time to live your life and accomplish some of your goals. Then have a child when you are emotionally, financially, spiritually, mentally and physically ready. It will be much more rewarding to share life with a man you love and the embodiment of that love, your children, together.

"Keep your freedom"

"Release your hatred and forgive others."

Why are we born
to those we despise
why are we born
to those we dislike
why are we born to the unsympathetic
the uncaring
the unkind
why are we born
to the show-ers
of public adoration
who give private hell
why are we born
only to be forgotten
and left in the hands of the law
why are we born
to the sniffers of coke
smokers of crack
why are we born
to die of their disease
where is our strength
where is our chance
why are we born
to those with no hope
who have no future
thus ending mine

why are we born
to live in the torture
of the perpetual question
why

The force that affects us the most throughout our lives are our emotions. Our life is guided by what we feel and how we perceive things. We can remember good moments and bad moments. But it is the focus on the bad moments, the painful times, that can have a serious effect on our lives.

There are many factors that allow people to harbor anger in their hearts. Many mothers do not realize the power they have over their children through the use of their words. A mother can define and shape her child's life. It is her words of encouragement or anger that children remember. It is what mothers believe about their children that will shape that child's life.

Many times the difference between a so-called failure and a success is the relationship they had with their mother. I know this from looking around at everyday situations and seeing how people deal with and respond to their mothers. A child that has been verbally hurt by his mother or father will never forget it. That child will remember the pain of those words. The pain will turn into anger as the child approaches adulthood and realizes the effect the parents had on the shaping of his or her life.

Another common, but often unspoken, way that we hold onto anger is if we dealt with sexual abuse at some point in our lives. A child whose childhood was interrupted by some disgusting person will never forget. And if the molester was a parent or relative, the pain goes even deeper.

It is so devastating to have these experiences thrown at you, especially when you're a child. You are defenseless and being taken advantage of. But as an adult, for your psychological well-being and the freeing of your soul you will have to release the pain.

Forgive is a strong word. So I would say release the anger, release the pain and let that person deal with what they did to you. Whatever anyone has ever done to you is not significant enough to affect your life at this point. You have to let them go. The pain, the anger, the hurt, the fears, everything, has to go. So that you may move on with your life. That you may love again. And trust again. You have to do these things. Just as you cannot allow anyone to define your life, you cannot allow anyone to cripple it either with fear or anger. It's simply not worth it. Your life is meant to be much more than this.

You are hurting and hindering yourself by holding onto the anger and pain. Take back the power of your life. Begin again, by releasing the hatred and anger and living this life for yourself.

Lesson: If you do not forgive, you will not grow. If you do not release hatred from your heart, you will close your life to the beauty and enjoyment of life and love.

"Don't complain if you're not willing to change."

Actions are louder than words
so although your mouth is moving
I ain't really hearing s—t
I've learned to tune out
whatever you spew
and stand back
to see what you do
your mouth is like quicksand
being drowned out
cause you're talking
but you ain't saying nothing
your mind is not moving
your body is not moving
you are stagnant
and getting on my f—g nerves
Actions are louder than words
Actions
are louder
than words
Hear Me?

There are countless women that complain about the state of their relationships, and the state of their lives, but they never do anything to change it. They will tell you how they need to go back to school, how they need to leave this man, how they need to do this and they need to do that. The one thing they need to stop doing is moaning and start moving.

No one wants to hear you say I'm going to do this and then watch as you do nothing. Not a true friend anyway. A true friend wants the best for you, especially your happiness. If life is stagnant or a relationship is dead, get out, move on. Sounds too simple? It isn't. You just say, this is enough, I'm out, and you leave.

The only thing holding these women back is themselves. They're blocking their own happiness. Holding back their life by sitting there talking and complaining. If you want so much out of life, if you want more, you're gonna have to work for it. You're gonna have to go for it. When your mouth is moving and your body's not, you're just wasting time. The years will pass by and you will still be saying my life shouldn't be like this, when all along you have the power to make life anything you want.

Lesson: Actions speak louder than words.

"Let your good deed speak for itself."

When it is truly felt
it is mine to give
how much or how little
it is my decision
based on what I feel I can
it is my desire to do more
not because of what you think
but because my soul cries
at the heartache of others
my spirit feels the pain
my heart remembers the loss

I am not too far from you
for I am human
and life has many changes
this was not planned
this was not planned
this was not planned
but maybe my one deed
that one smile
can help
to make you see
that life can always change
and people do care

Nothing takes away from an act of kindness more than a person who continually tells others, guess what I did? If in fact what you did was from your heart you do not have to and would not want to impress others with your act. Sure, there are times when you can't believe a situation was so bad and you tell your girls about it. But this situation is when you're really just saying look at me, look at the type of person I am.

Your heart speaks for you. You do not have to tell others what type of person you are. Your actions and character will speak for you. Do things that express your individuality and your love of humanity. Don't do things just to impress others. Don't do things just because it is the 'thing' to do. Do what feels right for you and leave it at that.

A little humility in the right situation will lead you to continue to do great acts and have those whom you help appreciate your loving spirit.

Lesson: An act of kindness should be an expression of your spirit, not an intention to impress.

"Design your life."

Like a piece of grass
that fits in the lawn
we are each a part
of life
and we each are distinct
it is a choice
to decide which way we will go
what turn we will make in life
the eternity of our lives
depends on our spirit
the connection we have made
the love we hold within

Everything in your life should be a reflection of you. It should consist of the person you are and wish to be. Friends should be an extension of you and able to help you grow. Every relationship should be healthy, loving and supportive.

Many times we hold onto things in our life for comfort. We're just used to this person or a certain situation. We have to know when to break the complacency and go on to the next level. There are levels of life and therefore levels of friendship. Every friendship is not going to last until your dying day. You have to know when a relationship is not beneficial to your life.

If you have a friend that you know would not be there for you in hard times, but you remain friends with her, you are limiting yourself. You are saying that your relationships don't have to give you much. You are willing to accept someone liking you rather than having a friend that loves and supports you no matter what. You are instilling a belief that people don't have to give you much and showing others that you do not expect much. That way no one has to go out of his or her way or do anything extraordinary to please you.

When you limit yourself to these type of friendships, you affect your whole life. You stop yourself from experiencing relationships based on friendship, honesty, trust and love. If you're not going to have these necessary components, you don't have a friendship. It will also affect your chances for a successful relationship.

You cannot allow yourself to excuse the behavior of others. Just by being aware of the situation does nothing. You have to be aware and eliminate the "friendship." Stop putting your life on hold by dealing with people who do not have your total best interests in hand. Obviously, they do not love you. You should surround yourself with a family of friends that love and support you.

When you decide who you will and will not spend time with and befriend, you gain control in other parts of your life as well. You will see that you will make better decisions and choices based on what's right for you. You will team up with people that have your interest and theirs in mind. Life won't seem like such a struggle when there are people that you know you can depend on.

Lesson: Knowing deep down that there are people that will be there for you in life because they care about you enables you to have more confidence in your everyday life.

"Be yourself"

"Respect is a simple thing."

If I have me
in full
and believe
in myself
I do not have to question
you
I do not care
I do not define
my life
based on you
because I am glorious
my god
I am me

Many young girls walk around thinking they know what respect is. But I think you have been misinformed. Respect is not an attitude that disrespects others. Respect is not an attitude that makes you think others are inferior to you. Respect is an inner belief based on loving yourself and having confidence. When you believe in yourself no one else affects you. You will not compare yourself or put others down. You will be happy with who you are and what you are capable of doing.

Respect is a simple thing. Give it and you will get it.

Respect is knowing I can, I will, I must, I am about yourself and not being capable of being swayed by anyone's opinion. When you have respect for yourself you realize that other people are important also. With self-respect you open your life to challenges, opportunities and learning experiences.

Lesson: Respect is something you will receive when you are willing to give it.

"Pushiness is not beautiful."

Choking
choking
choking
on your words
you're stuffing them down my throat
faster than I can swallow
a breath is needed
but you're not giving
you believe the stuff you're saying
without even stopping
or breathing
or listening
what is going on here
who is this woman
that thinks she knows
me
the world
everything
everyone
belittling
but really putting herself down
by closing herself up
in her own world
where she is queen
and no one else exists

and no one else wants to
they just look away
from afar
and say
that girl
is a fool

There are many women that feel they are a challenge to men because they speak their mind. Speaking your mind is in no way a bad thing. It is the way that you speak that can be the problem. What you have to understand is everyone is not intimidated by your aggressive and assertive behavior. You may just be working the last of their nerve.

A woman who thinks she knows everything and does not open herself to learning from others is a nuisance. There is no one in this world who knows everything. Each and every day of your life you should be learning. Every day. So instead of thinking you're a challenge, close your mouth and listen for awhile. You just may learn something.

When you can't listen, no one will listen to you. When you are not open to learning from those you debate with, they will not hear what you say either.

To get the most out of life you have to realize that life is a learning experience. That means that at any moment, at any time, you can learn something that will change your life. Anyone can be the teacher. You just have to have your life open to learning.

Lesson: Those that are always seeking to challenge and debate close their life to listening and learning from others and will remain stagnant until they learn that everyone is a teacher.

"Live your life without regret."

I never want to say
I wish
oh I wish
never want to say
I would have
I would have
I could have
really should have
I never want to say these things
never want to feel that pain
see the look of disappointment
on my own face
feel the tears glide down
as I realize the years have escaped
oh no
I can't do that to myself
my heart
would never forget
the pain
the life
the time
that was wasted

The last thing you want to do in life is look back and regret the choices you did or did not make. There is no way to go back, no way to correct life. Once a choice is made, it usually has lasting effects. So you have to look at your life and where you want to be clearly. Make decisions that will get you the most out of life.

It is very painful to look back on life and say, I wish I had done this or that. It's something I vowed I would never do to myself. I advise you to make the same vow and stick to it. This vow is not simple. You have to realize that when you say *I vow never to regret,* you are confirming that you will do things in your life. You will live life to the fullest. You will make decisions that enrich your life. You will do things that are new to you. You will try to create a life you will love. This is a commitment to yourself. It is a commitment you must make.

When you make a commitment to yourself you establish a certain level of achievement for yourself. There are things you will have to accomplish in order for your life to be fulfilled. Since you do not want to regret not seeking opportunities and challenges you will be more open to thinking in your best interest and making wise choices.

When you get off track in life, remember that there is a bigger purpose for your life that God knows. So although you may wonder why you did this or that. In the scheme of things it was meant to happen. Everything happens for a reason.

While your life and the fulfillment of it are the main focus, you also do not want to regret the way you did or did not treat others. It is important to treat others as you would want to be treated. When you accomplish things in life, give back to others in some way. Live a life that in the end you can say I loved, I lived, I laughed, I helped, I learned.

Lesson: Live your life in a way that you never have to look back and say I wish I could do this over.

"Use the doubt of others to push you forward."

When you tell me no
I look at you & laugh
you don't know me
like a rubber ball
I bounce higher
when pushed down
I will go farther
than you ever have
reach higher
than you ever dreamed
in spite of
you
in love of
myself
I will achieve
because I must
and for awhile
I will throw it in your face
and say ha ha
you never thought I'd see this place
I'll show you how happiness looks
on a well deserving face

If there is someone important to you that tends to put you down and doesn't believe you will achieve great things in life, take that energy, that anger, that fear, that pain you have and use it to make the best of your life. This should fuel you to want more and show others and yourself that you can accomplish whatever you put your mind to.

Whenever someone attempts to put you down or stifle your life, you have to take their ignorance and make it your power. If you want to mentally survive and make something of your life, you cannot let people have control over your mind or your life. It's kind of an *I'll show you* attitude. It's not a way to live your life forever, because eventually you won't care what they think. But until you get to that point, make sure that you turn this situation to your advantage and surpass their expectations.

Never have hate or anger in your heart for anyone. All it does is damage you. It stops you from achieving things. It stops you from loving. It stops you from living. Life will correct the pain a person has inflicted on you. It is not on you to make sure they hurt the way they hurt you. You control how you react and how this will affect your life. Above all else, control your life.

Lesson: When anyone attempts to put you down, take that as a challenge to push yourself towards your ultimate dreams.

"Don't hold onto problems."

Like a sickness it is
heart palpitations
racing heart
like a sickness it is
the blues are loved by many
survived by those
who believe themselves to be super
but I'm not super
I'm just me
and this is too much
my heart hurts too much
can't you see
don't you see
the pain in my eyes
can't you describe my life to me
why does this hurt me
who wished this upon me
did I do this to myself
no couldn't be
why is this hurting me
I need to release this
this pain
free me
from myself
before I go
insane

We always want to be in control of our lives. We always want to appear as if we have everything together, but no one has his or her life totally together. There are times when you will need others, even if it is just to talk. You have to know that problems are hard to bear when you bear them alone. Once you talk them over with a good friend you release some of the tension.

Talking to a good friend is therapeutic for you. It is a way to take the anger, pain or disappointment out of your body and into the world. If you hold onto problems and just wonder *why me?* it will affect your body and mind. Your body will experience pains and aches. You will begin to believe that only bad things happen to you.

In order to relieve stress you have to keep it real with yourself. You have to realize that all problems can be overcome or handled in some way. You just have to make sure you have good friends that you can talk with.

The more you focus on a problem the larger it seems and becomes. When you hold it to yourself and think only you can solve it you make the process of getting over it take much longer. Even when something seems so painful that you just couldn't tell anyone, you have to trust the love of your friends. Release the pain by sharing it, talking it through, with others. When you talk you will open yourself to feeling some love and receiving advice from friends. You will learn that you are not the first to deal with a difficult problem. You will see that problems last only as long as it takes to find a solution.

Lesson: You can overcome any problem when you are willing to face it and allow others to help you.

"Embrace Life"

"Be reliable."

Once you are disbelieved
there is no way of getting back
no one wants you
when your time can't be tracked
who cares what happened
this time
it's always the same
you make up things
as if others can't think
so absorbed with your self
you can't think of anything else
foolish
selfish
girl
no one wants your friendship
no one wants your time
it soured when they were waiting for you
waiting for you to be there
when you said you would

You know people that say they're going to be somewhere at a certain time and they show up hours later. Or when they're supposed to do something they never show up and continue to give the same tired excuses. You do not want to be one of these people and you want to avoid them at all costs.

No one has respect for a person that doesn't do what they say they're going to do. You cannot excuse this away and just say it's part of that person's personality. It's disrespectful and will not change until you state that it is unacceptable. This person really has no respect for your time or friendship.

When you make a commitment to do something, follow through. If you say you are going to do something or be somewhere, do it. When someone is depending on you be there for them. Don't try to be everything to everyone but at least be true to your word.

Being reliable is showing people that you care about them, their friendship, and that you can be depended on. It is showing that you appreciate relationships and can honor commitments. Whether or not you are reliable is a strong indicator of the type of person, worker, and friend you are. If you are not reliable, people will even begin to question the things you say. You will not be believable. Also when you need someone to be there for you they may decide not to just to give you a taste of your own treatment.

Lesson: A reliable person is deemed as trustworthy, dependable and concerned for the well-being of others. Being reliable is being there for someone when they need you.

"Never underestimate yourself."

Every choice you have made
is right for you
you did what you knew
what you felt
you made the right choice
don't look down
don't give up
the power of God is within you
guiding you
to a life you deserve

As a friend of mine says, every choice is right if you used all the facts and knowledge you had at the time to make the best decision. You can accept this thinking because you need to believe it and because it's true. You are not making mistakes, you are living life.

You have to know that even with your perceived flaws, single parent, not pretty enough, not smart enough, etc., you are good enough for anyone in this worldm, because God made you. And I'm telling you to believe, *know,* you are the best and people need to be worthy of you. You are that special. You are that important. You are a gift to them. Remember that.

Don't limit your life. Don't close your life. Don't end your life with thoughts that bring you emotionally and mentally down.

Life can be a wonderful experience if you open yourself up to it. If you are beautiful (on the inside), loving, spiritual, caring, and giving, people will want to be around you. It is who we are, who we believe we are, how we are that will bring us what we want, need and deserve in this life.

There is someone for everyone. There is a wonderful life waiting for you. If you want it, want it, you can have it. Do not think even for a moment that you don't deserve something or someone. You deserve the best.

Lesson: Never stop believing in yourself or the power of God.

"Don't put others down."

I believe we are all one
cept for you
you don't even know where to shop
reject
what are you thinking
that I would even dare speak to you
excuse me
do you think we have something in common
I'm far better
than you
please excuse you
do you know what condescend means
I don't have time enough
to do that
so don't even bother speaking to me
I am busy getting in tune
with my spirituality

I had a friend who would always put people down. She didn't notice it, and at the time I didn't tell her, because she actually thought she was a loving, caring, spiritual person. But she would judge people based on their material possessions or their life achievements.

Let me tell you if you put someone else down you are putting yourself down. When I say believe in yourself, believe you are the best. I mean that. But that does not mean that you are better than someone. We all have the spirit of God in us, every last one of us, from a homeless person to a billionaire. We are all the same spirit. We all want love, we all want to be appreciated, we all want to be needed.

No one is better because of any material possession, color or education. If you are a spiritual person, you do not compare yourself to others or put them down. You do not believe you are better in any way.

Putting others down is literally a disgusting quality. It sounds ugly coming from you. If you were in a bad or poor situation, you would not want someone to put you down because of the way you looked. Instead you would hope someone would have heart enough to acknowledge you and say hi.

Until you feel how wrong it is to treat others badly, until you know deeply that it is wrong to put others down for any reason, until you can look at everyone and say there but for the grace of God go I, you are not living to your full potential. You do not have a true connection with God. God sees the beauty, the spirit, the love in everyone. And as a part of God you should be able to do the same. Believe me, it's not difficult. It's just opening your mind.

Now, when I say love, I do not mean that you love everyone. That's not honest. What it is saying is that everyone is capable of receiving the love of God. Therefore, you have no right to put them down. God is within them, just as he is within you.

Lesson: Watch what you proclaim. Make sure you are who you say you are.

"Share your love"

"Pleasing everyone is a fool's paradise."

Running

running running

around

trying to please my man

my child

my boss

my mother

my father

the stranger on the street

whew I'm tired

ain't got no more to give

oh jesus

I forgot to give to myself

Let's be clear. You cannot, cannot, cannot please everyone. And God knows you shouldn't try. Trying to please everyone is like a dog running around trying to catch his tail. It's never going to work out.

When you try to please everyone, you feel like a puppet on a string. Like you're running around trying to catch your breath. It's an unhappy, miserable state of being that will stop the minute you say, Look you do this yourself. I'm telling you you're gonna have to go there.

Black women especially have this thing with being a superwoman. We can do this, we can do that. Honey, look, what I may be able to do is one thing. What I'm gonna do is another thing. Life is about me enjoying it, not pleasing others. This is what you're going to have to know.

Your creed should be: I will do for you what I can, but I will not do more than that. Always give your best, of course. But know when to say *when*. When you ration your time, you have more energy to do the things you want to do. You give yourself a break in between tasks. And you have time to relax.

I'm known for my long bubble baths. You know why? Because "me time" is very necessary. Dishes, mail, phone, all that can wait. I sit myself down and recoup. I'm not gonna stress for anyone. I'm not going to try and make up for "lost time." I'm not going to try and act like I can do everything at anytime. Oh no, I know when to say I'll pass or I'll do this later. Because stress will kill you. You have to know how to relax and when to say no.

There are many ways to be happy. Trying to please others all the time is not one of them. Imagine someone hammering you in the head. That's what you'll feel like if you try to be everything to everyone. Avoid that. Control your life, by controlling your time and your mind.

Lesson: Overextending yourself can take a toll on your body, your mind and your spirit. Control your life by being realistic about what you can and cannot do for others. Know when to rejuvenate yourself by relaxing and doing things for you.

Stop and Run

Do
what you always do
& you'll get the same s—t
change a thought
you might be surprised
life is what you are willing to make it

In life we can get stuck. We can get set in our ways, and lose our focus. But somewhere, somehow, we can still see the hazy picture. We can still see that life should be different. We could somehow be different. What you have to do then is stop whatever it is you're doing and run in the right direction.

You have to change the way you think, the way you react, the way you go after things. You don't want to always do the same thing because then you will always get the same result. So you're going to have to switch cycles and change your life into what you want it to be. To do that sometimes you have to find another way, a better way.

The only way you're going to make a change in your life is when you want it more than anything. You have to break the mold you're stuck in and live life, try life, another way. This isn't to say you're life is bad or miserable. It's just saying if it doesn't feel totally right maybe you should stop and look at your options. Stop and look at what you've been doing and what you could be doing. A rut is the bed of hell. You never want to enter it. You never want life to just go the same way every day. Life is a journey. You should enjoy it.

Take a breath. Take the chance. And find new things to do with your life. Find ways to challenge and enrich your life. Find the things you love to do and incorporate those into your life. Don't get stuck doing something you don't even like for the rest of your life. You should love what you do. Hear what I'm saying: you should love what you do. How many people do that? How many people honestly want that?

The difference between honestly wanting and wanting is the desire. If you honestly want it you're gonna find every way to make it happen. If you just want something, you're just dreaming, just wasting time. But wanting something honestly, strongly, is like hunger. You have to fulfill that need. You have to live life to the fullest. That's the only way to enjoy it. That's the only way to love it.

Lesson: You must never lose your desire for life, or the want of a better life. It can be realized if you just change your methods and focus.

Money, money, money

"Dreams need finance"

From the first week, from your first paycheck, save. Find out about automatic investment plans from mutual fund companies and at least put away the minimum fifty dollars a month. This will pay off for you in the end. You may not think it's much, but it will add up. You have to be prepared for your future. You have to be able to invest in you.

Watch yourself with the credit cards. God knows, there's a lot of sisters with bad credit. My best advice is don't use them if you don't have to. Don't be swayed by the free soda on college campus. Don't be enticed by the low introductory rate. How often would you walk into a bank and ask for a loan, with the highest possible interest rate they have? That's what you do every time you use a credit card.

If you have dreams of buying a house, watch yourself with the credit. Don't indulge to feel better. Don't indulge because you just need that shirt. Keep it real with yourself and use what you have until you can pay cash. Credit really should only be for big ticket items. A computer or something. But not for your everyday maintenance.

Money is a necessary tool. You need it to get things you want in life. So make sure you save and spend wisely.

Lesson: Money, like emotions, is something you must control to keep your life on the right track.

"Share your knowledge."

If you know when & where
share that
help a sister out
let me know what you know
so we can keep the legacy
in tact
spread the knowledge
like wisdom was carried on our back
take it from railroad philosophy
we all need to get there
some are just more aware
of the stars
spread what you know
help a sister out

There's nothing more annoying than a person that has a wealth of knowledge and doesn't share it with the community. If you want the people in the community to be empowered, if you want your community to make better decisions and choices, if you want your community to be powerful, and you have ideas, knowledge and wisdom to share, get out there and help. Start a class. Start a workshop. Each one, teach one has to be a motto.

People need and want help and sometimes the only way they'll get it is if you jump in and help. Why acquire knowledge if you're not going to share it? Please God, get out there and help somebody learn. Teach somebody what you know. Don't sit up in the house saying the community is going downhill when you could be helping someone, even one person, get their life on track. It's just not excusable and should be totally unacceptable to you.

It's really horrible how much of our history is stored up in people's brains. Share your experiences. Share them with the community. Children need to know. The community needs to know.

Lesson: Never go so far that you don't know how to go back and give back.

A Special Poem For You

I am
> my own best friend
> my own strength

I am
> being pushed
> molded
> into a beautiful
> loving
> inspirational

woman
I define my life
> God defines my life

I am God's love
> manifest

in human form
I will
use the power of God
> that resides in me

to create a life
I Love
> I will give that legacy

of loving myself
> to my children

and all that I know
God is within me
> I will never forget that

God is within me
      I can get through
      accomplish
      be
      Anything
      that I want to be
I am
      my own strength
      my own friend
my own love
I am
complete
      and powerful
I am beautiful
      because my spirit
      is based in love

Life Lessons
The Complete List

1. Learn from your experiences.
2. Be open to opportunities.
3. Do not give up on yourself.
4. Go for your highest goal.
5. Believe in yourself.
6. Treat others as you would want to be treated.
7. Your expectations determine your reality.
8. Don't play games with the men you become involved with.
9. Don't expect a man to complete your life.
10. Don't concentrate on marriage; focus on having a loving relationship.
11. Don't tell too much about your man.
12. Be aware of your surroundings.
13. Be the Chooser, Not the Chosen.
14. Think about the impact of your decisions before you make them.
15. Notice the subtle clues in your relationships.
16. Don't try to fix anyone.
17. Don't think you can replace or appease the problems your man is having with his family.
18. Love yourself first.
19. Treat your children as precious spirits.
20. Don't fall for love, walk into it with your eyes and heart open.
21. Mama doesn't always know best.
22. The best pain is no pain.
23. Release your negativity and hatred of others.
24. Determine your life, make a life plan.
25. Judge a person on their character and actions, not their words.
26. Don't love for potential, love for right now.
27. Don't get caught up in the moment. Think before you react or act.

28. You can learn from anyone, at any time.
29. Don't envy, emulate.
30. You are what you believe.
31. Make yourself beautiful.
32. Be a role model.
33. You have the power to change the world.
34. What you do will come back to you.
35. Do not lower your standards or your values for anybody.
36. Bitterness will eat away your heart.
37. Be sure you know both sides of a story before you pick a side.
38. Be sure your first is the one you really love.
39. Don't do what you will regret later.
40. Separate the emotions from the facts to make your decisions.
41. Listen to your heart, think with your brain.
42. Never let anyone abuse you in any way.
43. Your spirit is your motivation.
44. Look at the beauty in life.
45. Cherish your life.
46. At any moment, you have the capability of changing your life.
47. Risk is the food of life, it will help you grow.
48. Know what you want out of relationships.
49. Confidence is not an attitude, it's a state of mind.
50. Appreciate where you are.
51. Know who you are.
52. Know your definition of success and happiness.
53. Stick to your values.
54. Do not try to break your man's spirit or change him into what you want him to be.
55. Choose your battles wisely.
56. Expand your horizons-travel, take classes, read.
57. Be careful of becoming stagnant.
58. Think about the feelings of your friends.
59. Keep some things to yourself.
60. Make life work for you.
61. Know when to listen.
62. Strive to do well at whatever you do or don't do it at all.
63. Appreciate and love yourself.

64. Demand respect through your actions.
65. Exceed the expectations of others.
66. Don't judge yourself or limit yourself by what others believe or perceive of you.
67. You cannot make someone love you, you have to be someone who can be loved.
68. People will try to block your light (blessings) and steal your energy.
69. The only influence a person can exert over you is the amount you allow them.
70. Misery loves company.
71. Don't let anyone steal your thunder.
72. Love freely so you can receive free unconditional love.
73. Don't place your hangups on somebody else.
74. Don't wait for someone else to make your life better.
75. You are the most important person in the world.
76. God is everywhere, you just have to open your eyes.
77. Before you begin your quest for Mr. Right make sure you're Ms. Right.
78. Be realistic about your relationships, treat him too!
79. Struggle is part of your spiritual evolution.
80. Make sure you are ready for every opportunity.
81. You have to work for what you want.
82. You have to have control of your life.
83. Anyone who can dictate what you do with your life is stifling your spirit and stunting your growth.
84. Give of yourself because it is the spiritual thing to do.
85. Cherish your spirit, feed your spirit.
86. Learn how to forgive.
87. God gives you advice through your intuition.
88. When you listen to your heart (inner voice) you will be happy.
89. Don't give more than you are getting.
90. Never give up on yourself.
91. Life is meant to be fulfilling.
92. Every decision matters.
93. Abusive relationships come in many forms.
94. Become a person you love, then share that love.
95. Confront your destiny-find out who you are.

96. Know your past.
97. Your career choice is your life choice.
98. Use your fear to your advantage.
99. God is within you, you are within God.
100. Know what you want out of life.
101. Know what you will and will not stand for.
102. Know when to end friendships.
103. Choose a career.
104. Honor your friendships.
105. Look for your inspiration.
106. Never surrender to life.
107. People are watching your actions.
108. Be real with yourself and with others.
109. Deal with your relationships honestly and openly.
110. Don't be afraid of love.
111. Have sex when you are emotionally and spiritually ready.
112. Save, save, save some money.
113. You define your happiness and your success.
114. Be aware of the lessons in life.
115. Stay focused on your goals.
116. Live on your own, at least once.
117. Do not put others down.
118. Do not let anyone tell you what to do with your life.
119. Be careful of the people who don't have nothing, because they'll want your something.
120. Take responsibility for your life.
121. Release your hatred, forgive others.
122. Look for opportunities to love.
123. Help others.
124. Recognize your need to change and grow.
125. Recognize your spiritual duty and do it.
126. Seek ways to improve yourself.
127. Break bad habits and addictions.
128. Learn how to live with loss.
129. Decide to find happiness within yourself.
130. Share your knowledge.
131. Be strong in what you believe in.

132. Love what you do.
133. Don't be influenced by others.
134. Be aware of people's motivations.
135. Know when to move on.
136. Life is a journey; enjoy every moment.
137. Men love independent women.
138. Create success for yourself.

My Life

I've been through so many things that I've become my own best friend, my own strength. I tell myself what I need to hear. I inspire myself. I remind myself of how special I am.

I know that with all the lessons God has given me there is an ultimate reason. There will be a day when I can say that's why that happened. I know he's not giving up on me. Just pushing me, molding me, to become the person I need to be.

God is the only one I will allow to define my life. I am in no way a religious person. I don't go to church. God's presence though is strongly within me, inside my heart. I try to give that pure love to others. I try to show people how much I love and care about them. I want people in my life to know they are loved. And I'll be there for them when they need me. I love them completely.

My strength to get through life is fueled by my desire and my love. I want a better life; therefore, I can't allow anyone to hurt the process. I need to be happy. I need to be me. So I can never stop and let life get to me. I can't sit for long and say *why me?* I can never tell myself there's no way of getting out of this.

I will always find a way to achieve, to love, to be me. I have to! It is as essential to me as my breath. God gave me so much that I have to give something back.

I have to show God that I appreciate the life he gave me. And I will become that person I am destined to be. I will fulfill every dream, one step at a time. I will never close my mind to life or love.

I will feel the moment. I will feel the pain, the joy, the heartache, the love, the crying, the laughing. I will feel life. Live it to its fullest. So I can be fulfilled, and give my love. There's no other way for me to be.

My dreams are the precious essence of my mind. My talent is my strength. The love I can give is beautiful because I love myself so much.

No one can hurt me more than I can hurt myself. No one will ever abuse or use me. It's unacceptable. My life will not be defined by that.

Even at my weakest moment, I am my best strength. I have the power to shape my life. I have the love to heal my heart. I have the ability to change everything.

God is within me and I will never forget that. God is within me and I can get through anything, accomplish anything, be anything that I want to be.

I am my own strength. My own friend. My own love. So I never lose because I have me.

We are all complete in that way. We just have to feel it. Remember it. Honor it. We have everything we need inside of us.

We are the love of God manifest in human form. We are so powerful. We just need to know it.

Everything you need is inside of you. Bring it out. Bring out the God. Bring out the love. Acknowledge your spirit.

Always remember, spirituality is not saying you're better than others. It is not turning your back on your fellow man. It is not about putting others down or judging or limiting them to your expectations.

Spirituality is opening your heart to love and allowing yourself to learn from every individual. It is knowing that God wants the best for you, that God is within you—and everybody else—and therefore you can make the world a better place by simply being you and allowing God to flow through you and touch the lives of others.

I wish you the very best on your search for the most powerful love, the love that is inside of you. I hope you find it one day and realize how magnificent you are.

Take care.

Peace & Love,
Natasha

I would love to hear from you, email: Tasha626@excite.com or check out www.lifeyoulove.com for contact and other project information.

About the Author

Natasha Munson is an award-winning poet and writer. Her work has been included in many anthologies and she was nominated for Poet of the Year 1998. She is a sought-after motivational speaker with her focus on spirituality and empowerment. Natasha has sponsored many programs for children including, *Black Child Expo*. She is currently designing the national Black Women's Empowerment Workshop and accompanying journal.